D1706048

Father Fidelis Mukonori S.J.

THE GENESIS
OF VIOLENCE IN ZIMBABWE

THE HOUSE OF BOOKS
HARARE 2015

First published in Zimbabwe
by The Centre for Peace Initiatives in 2011
47 Mcmeekan Road, Milton Park
Harare, Zimbabwe
www.cpia.org.zw

This Edition published by
The House of Books
8 Redhill Road, Highlands
Harare, Zimbabwe

ISBN 978 0 7974 6535 0

Production and Editorial
Dimitrije Unkovski

Transcript and Edit
Grace Mutandwa

Graphic Designer
Dunja Pantic (www.thedunja.com)

Printing and Binding
MG Printers
Harare, Zimbabwe

THE GENESIS OF VIOLENCE IN ZIMBABWE

Father Fidelis Mukonori, S. J. was born in Zimbabwe in 1947. He holds a Masters of Theology (MTH) degree from Berkeley, California, USA, a Diploma in Social Development, Canada, a Diploma in Philosophy, Zimbabwe, and an Advanced Certificate in Conflict Resolutions, South Africa.

He has been a member of the Catholic Commission for Justice and Peace since 1974. From 1975 he worked with Silveira House as Youth Coordinator, Youth Director, Leadership and Civics Trainer and Internal Auditor. He served as Provincial of the Jesuits in Zimbabwe.

Currently he is Parish Priest for Chishawasha, Principal of Chishawasha Primary Boarding School and Executive Director for the Centre for Peace Initiatives in Africa.

CONTENTS

FOREWORD

Using a broad brush on a small canvas, the author deftly paints a disturbing picture of recurring violence in Zimbabwe, from pre-colonial times dating back as far back as 1879. Father Fidelis Mukonori S.J. has combined research, his training as a Roman Catholic priest and the age-old African tradition of story-telling, to give the reader insights into the genesis of violence in Zimbabwe.

The material is handled with candour, sensitivity, and simplicity, characteristic of a man of the cloth. Not only are the events explained in their historical, economic and social contexts, they also include poignant cameos, anecdotes from the author's grandmother and his own personal encounters with violence or potentially violent situations, as a young man growing up in Southern Rhodesia and as an adult in Rhodesia and Zimbabwe.

Why a book on violence? That is a legitimate question. The Centre for Peace Initiatives in Africa (CPIA) did not commission Father Mukonori to write a book so as to encourage violence or open up old wounds. His training and position in society would not allow him to be associated with such a project anyway! CPIA's main objective is to discuss ways and means of moving Zimbabwe from a culture of violence to a culture of peace as well as to promote and optimize dialogue, so as to achieve and con-solidate sustainable peace, stability and security in Zimbabwe.

This noble objective can only be achieved through dialogue and reconciliation. And reconciliation is only possible if what happened in the past is told honestly and truthfully. It is for this reason that we believe Father Mukonori's booklet is a useful ad-dition to the tools required in the process of preventing political, economic and social conflicts and promoting peace.

Admittedly, there are many books - big volumes - on the subject of violence in Zimbabwe, but we don't know of a book that specifically focuses on per-se. CPIA hopes to produce other booklets on different topics annually, all with a common aim: prevention of conflicts and promotion of peace. Father Mukonori's booklet is the first in the series.

CPIA would like to thank Father Mukonori for taking the time from an incredibly busy schedule to sit down and write this booklet.

Dr. Leonard T. Kapungu
Former Executive Director
Centre for Peace Initiatives in Africa

ACKNOWLEDGEMENTS

The Centre for Peace Initiatives in Africa (CPIA) is a regional peace organization based in Harare, Zimbabwe. It works towards a stable and peaceful Zimbabwe and Africa at large and is characterised by sustainable peace, development and good governance.

CPIA realises this vision and mission by:

- Undertaking applied research and training;
- Working collaboratively with various stakeholders;
- Facilitating dialogue workshops at various levels; and
- Collecting and interpreting information.

The Centre for Peace Initiatives in Africa (CPIA) remains indebted to those who assisted in this project. In particular, the CPIA wishes to thank Frederick Sadomba who spent much of his time assisting Father Mukonori in developing the manuscript. CPIA also thanks Ms. Rena Chitombo-Zvandasara who endured uneven tempers but still helped in typing the book. Last but not least the CPIA acknowledges the invaluable assistance it received from the National Archives of Zimbabwe, which provided sources that assisted in the research of the book.

[1]   A shoot will spring from the stock of Jesse, a new shoot will grow
from his roots.

[2]   On him will rest the spirit of Yahweh, the spirit of wisdom and
insight, the spirit of counsel and power, the spirit of knowledge and fear
of Yahweh:

[3]   his inspiration will lie in fearing Yahweh. His judgement will not
be by appearances. his verdict not given on hearsay.

[4]   He will judge the weak with integrity and give fair sentence for the
humblest in the land. He will strike the country with the rod of his
mouth and with the breath of his lips bring death to the wicked.

[5]   Uprightness will be the belt around his waist, and constancy the belt
about his hips.

[6]   The wolf will live with the lamb, the panther lie down with the kid,
calf, lion and fat-stock beast together, with a little boy to lead them.

[7]   The cow and the bear will graze, their young will lie down together.
The lion will eat hay like the ox.

[8]   The infant will play over the den of the adder; the baby will put his
hand into the viper's lair.

[9]   No hurt, no harm will be done on all my holy mountain, for the
country will be full of knowledge of Yahweh as the waters cover the sea.

[10]   That day, the root of Jesse, standing as a signal for the peoples, will
be sought out by the nations and its home will be glorious.

INTRODUCTION

The people of Zimbabwe are renowned for their patience, discipline, reliability, hard working and are generally peace-loving. Sometimes such attributes of being peace loving may be misconstrued by other people as a sign of docility. In recent times, however, Zimbabweans have surprised the world by showing traits of fearlessness, willingness to challenge and sadly, propensity for violence, particularly when the country is facing a national election.

The levels of violence have reached such alarming proportions considering that Zimbabweans are the same people who love peace, tranquillity and enjoy going about their daily business in so many enterprising ways. It appears there must be something that ignited events in the history of Zimbabwe, which aroused their survival instincts. The booklet seeks to track the society's history which moulded Zimbabweans into the present nation state, with the view to discover the origins and possible causes of such violent tendencies that left a trail of murder, mayhem and gaping emotional wounds. The ultimate objective is to find a way forward through instilling and affirming national reconciliation among all the people of Zimbabwe, regardless of ethnicity, colour or creed.

This book is a historical perspective covering the period from 1879 to 1890, then continuing from 1893 to 1897 and to the Second Republic, 2009.

At the outset, it is necessary to define two terms, 'Violation' and 'Violence.' Violation means an infringement of the customary practices and breaking laws of the country. It also means wilful disregard of the rule of law as prescribed by domestic laws of the nation. Violation begets more violence if it is left uncontrolled.

Violence could be defined as an activity marked by extreme force or sudden intense activities so furious to the point of being improper and unjust. Violence also has to do with physical acts of causing extreme pain to the victim. There are other types of violence but for the purposes of this book, the definition of violence is that it takes various forms according to different situations. These various definitions will enable easier interpretations of how Violation and Violence manifest themselves in Zimbabwe. To give a precise definition of violence would be a mammoth task but for all practical purposes a working definition would suffice.

EARLY FORMS AND USE OF INSTITUTIONALISED VIOLENCE

Violence in its various forms has occurred all over the world since time immemorial when tribes fought each other in internecine tribal wars. This chapter focuses on how institutionalized violence occurred. For instance, the issue of how indigenous people were treated right from the beginning of colonization. When foreigners conquered the country and took definite political positions, and exercised their power and sovereignty over the local people, this was in itself a violation of the local inhabitants and their existence as a nation which already existed. It has to be stated from the outset that the locus of the violence is in the nature and behaviour of the white people who occupied the country. The Berlin conference of 1884 set in motion an aggressive scramble for territorial land grab by colonialists, who particularly victimized the indigenous African people. This set in motion a "strange bed fellowship between the indigenous black majority and the minority settler white communities" who shared a living in colonial Southern Rhodesia from 1890 onwards (Tapfumaneyi, A. W, unpublished seminar paper, 1999). Present day Zimbabwe was not immune from this territorial violence as the country was later occupied by whites through force.

Violence as a policy to control local people was an act of misdirected aggressive impulse, selfishness, hatred and lust for power. The other causes become incidental and should be interpreted in the light of the factors mentioned earlier.

The genesis of the British Colony called Rhodesia was in September 1890 after the Pioneer Column sponsored by Cecil John Rhodes forced its way into the territory using violence, racism and force creating antagonism between the two main population groups, namely the whites and the blacks. The reasons for the conquest and occupation of underdeveloped and militarily weaker societies by the industrial nations were complex. During that period, in imperial Europe, there was plenty of heady talk about the progress of mankind and the spread of civilization. Europeans were inspired by contemporary Social-Darwinism and the new imperialism which convinced them that it was the destiny of the Anglo-Saxon races to civilize the world. Nothing could withstand the force of that conviction, certainly not the rights of those who stood in its way.

The British Empire was described as infinite – *where the sun never sets*. Whites who joined the Pioneer Column intended to establish a Second Rand in Zimbabwe in the wake of the discovery of gold in the Transvaal in 1867. In order to do that, the British South Africa Company (BSAC) obtained a Royal Charter from the metropolis, London. Just like its contemporaries, the Royal Niger Company, the North Borneo Company, the BSAC represented a revival of 17th century private enterprise, colonization and trading. The colonial power obtained a distant over-lordship of the territory cheaply, since the day-to-day administration; security and policing were in the hands of the company staff. The Charter was thus a legal instrument from the British empowering the BSAC to act on behalf of the colonizing power in investing in and administering the newly acquired territory. Thus from the onset there was institutionalized violence.

In 1890 a well armed Pioneer Column numbering 196 Pioneers and 500 police arrived in the land they were later to name Rhodesia. (Chitiyo, K, unpublished seminar paper, 1999). The column was heavily armed with machine-guns and artillery. The event which eventually ensued (in just ten years) paralleled those which had been played in North America during the previous two centuries. Trudging on in a somewhat single file, towards Mazowe, where gold had been discovered, the Column established strategic forts on the border with Bechuanaland. These forts were established at Tuli, Victoria, Enkeldorn and finally Salisbury. The Column reached Salisbury on 21 September 1890 where they hoisted the Union Jack.

From the foregoing, violence and violation became institutionalized. Right from the beginning, white Rhodesians stuck to the principle that war was an act of legalized violence intended to force black people to submit to the will of the white man. In the process, violence was the means of compulsory submission or subjugation of the blacks to the marauding Europeans.

Thus right from the beginning, the Rhodesian white regime believed that violence was a means to an end. Brutal force was used to expropriate the land from the local inhabitants. The whites did that because they actually believed they were doing so legally. The Royal Charter only mandated the pioneers to farm and mine in Mashonaland, where mineral and settlement rights had been granted by King Lobengula who was not aware of the pioneers' expansionist and imperialist aims.

The Rudd Concession of 30th October 1888, which Lobengula fruitlessly made petitions to Queen Victoria, the Royal Charter of 29th October 1889 effectively transformed the BSAC from a simple group of speculators into a strong commercial set up. Two Dukes one of them related to the royal family joined the board of directors of BSAC. The inclusion of these Dukes, and one of them being a member of the royal family was a sign of endorsing institutionalized violation and institutionalized violence in the colony. Therefore, it is essential to note that such kind of interference by imperial powers into the affairs of weaker territories was intended to conquer the weak ones and dislodge them from sovereign control, making institutionalized violence unacceptable.

Over many years, such incursions have always been swept under the carpet because the super powers always had the upper hand. History was distorted to suit the white man. Those who came as visitors, ended up as victors through deceit and violence. That influenced the narration of history which portrayed negatively the vanquished. That is the same issue with the history of Zimbabwe. Much of it was written according to those who conquered Zimbabwe, militarily, politically and worst of all, economically.

The Rudd Concession of 30th October 1888 envisaged a perpetual friendship with Britain. However, the friendship was lopsided as the whites would benefit more as compared to King Lobengula and the blacks. Rhodes had an imperial vision. Thus from the early 1890s the history of the then Southern Rhodesia became that of land seizure, alienation, anger and resentment.

Lobengula did not understand the technicalities of this language, especially what certain phrases meant, particularly those phrases which stated that the company had full power to do all the things that they might deem necessary. Cecil John Rhodes did not however, clarify all the details on paper and this was used to trick and take advantage of the trusting Lobengula. With that piece of paper, Rhodes thought he had all the powers to take over the whole country. He did not care about the violation perpetrated against the local people. In exchange King Lobengula received one thousand rifles and one hundred rounds of ammunition, a salary of 200 pounds a month and the promise of a boat which never arrived.

When Lobengula was later warned by his people of the consequences of such a Treaty with Rhodes, he was outraged and sent a messenger to Queen Victoria in England to protest. The Queen dismissed the complaint on the grounds that what had been signed had been sealed and therefore, could not be reversed. Lobengula had lost to the British. (Chitiyo, K. unpublished seminar paper, 1999).

On 6th May 1890, Rhodes gathered some volunteer white men known as the Freebooters. These were young white men of Anglo Saxon breed who had left Britain in search of employment and a better future in South Africa. They had little education and no profession but they were tough enough to take a gamble in life. In modern times they could be compared to mercenaries. The difference being that mercenaries are trained soldiers of fortune. These 180 young men were trained as soldiers to accompany 500 British South Africa Company Police (BSAP), destined for Salisbury, which is now Harare.

The BSAP Force was induced to believe that there could never be peace in Mashonaland and Matabeleland until the blacks were either exterminated or driven back to the African hinterland. The Chartered Company was thus given political mastery over a territory the size of France. The column then disbanded its members and began to look for prospects in trade, mining and later farming.

There was no agreement between the inhabitants of Mashonaland on what the new settlers would be doing. According to Rhodes, the treaty they had with Lobengula stated that Mashonaland and any other part of the country were all dominions under King Lobengula. This was not true. Rhodes had his vision to make sure that he was going to turn the country into another British colony.

Much to the chagrin of white pioneers, the Second Rand did not materialize as very little gold was discovered as had been anticipated by Rhodes and his colleagues. The pioneer column was disbanded and speedily transformed themselves into land grabbers. They were allowed to peg off large tracts of land.

In founding the new State, the Company needed to attract more settlers, but it did not have legal authority to parcel out land or issue legitimate Titles to Land. By 1893, the BSAC embarked on settling pioneers on 1 284 hectare "farms". From the start, there was no obligation imposed by the BSAC on the Pioneers over use of the land. The sole obligation was to pay an annual rent of $1 per year. These land grabs brought the settlers into direct and protracted collision with indigenous Shona and Ndebele customs and practices.

Traditionally, land, according to Shona custom was held sacrosanct and common heritage of the community, operating at family, clan, and village levels. Chiefs presided over land distribution. Further, the King and his chiefs had direct power with respect to land allocation. Similarly, both clans strongly believed that the real custodians of the land were the ancestors and that certain pieces of land were sacred. It was this clash of cultures between the whites, who had institutionalized violence and violation, and indigenous Africans who regarded land as both a material and cultural resource that would dominate Zimbabwean history before and after independence.

However, the main thrust of the 1893 war, was to drive the indigenous people into reserves. The "ordained destiny" was Mashonaland. However, unlike Australia and America (where the Aborigines and Red Indians) were nearly exterminated, the Ndebele and Shona were not vanquished. They were channelled into arid, poor overcrowded and dreary land which forced them to be perpetually dependent on the whites.

The 1893 war between white settlers and Amandebele, also dubbed The Matabele Rebellion, was shortly followed by the First Chimurenga War (1896-97), which many historical texts referred to as the Shona Rebellion. Although this clash was mainly a revolt against the seizure of land, primarily, it was exacerbated by a law that required blacks to pay hut tax.

Other causes of the 1893 war were:

- Dispossession of local people of their land;
- Forced labour and job reservation;
- Lack of respect and violation of people's way of life;
- High Taxation; and
- Racial Discrimination.

These measures were inimical to the Africans and severe enough to lead many into the First Chimurenga war.

It has to be noted that as of the 1893 Anglo-Ndebele war, the First Chimurenga War and the Second Chimurenga (1963 – 1980), the indigenous fighters were regarded as rebels or terrorists. It was not considered that they were fighting for their own dignity and in defence of not only their fatherland but its resources as well.

Thus in the First Chimurenga, colonial police and soldiers seized crops and livestock from the locals. That war was so brutal and violent that 8 000 lives were lost (Ranger, T. O, 1970), the locals were defeated and the whites entrenched themselves in power. The whites having created a colonial state, in the process institutionalised the land problem with which all successive governments were to grapple without success.

Very little is spoken of the violent nature of these wars especially among people who were taught history prior to Independence in 1980. It was history narrated and written through the eyes of the conquerors and not through the eyes of the conquered. Therefore violence committed against the people who were conquered was hardly mentioned or reported. What is very sad is that those issues to do with what was considered as a "native" way of life were considered barbaric.

Few historians have attempted to put Zimbabwe's history

into the right perspective. In this book there is reference to some issues which were originally left out. In this chapter there is the issue of speculation and violence. Violence had to go with deceit on the part of Rhodes and his colleagues; trickery and the telling of half truths.

The new land allocation policy of 1905 created about 60 Native Reserves (NRs) occupying about 22 percent of Rhodesia. Nearly all the African population of 700 000 now lived in the impoverished reserves. By then, the locals had lost about 16 million hectares of land to the whites that by 1920, the NRs constituted an area of 8.7 million hectares. According to Palmer, the number of settlers' farms (Freehold) reached 2 500 Farms swallowing an acreage of about 16 million hectares. (Chitiyo, K. unpublished seminar paper, 1999).

Besides the racial polarisation of land, land use also generated many conflicts between the blacks and the settlers. The settlers hated and were contemptuous of the indigenous and traditional land use. Africans were regarded as destructive farmers as they practiced the "slash and burn" method of farming. Once again, the colonial administration ignored the fact that deep ploughing methods were actually more destructive to the soil than the African way of cultivation. The colonial regime went on to accept and recommend the Alvord's methods on "centralisation" as a means of environmental and soil conservation. The training of African land demonstrators (madhumeni) was commenced and intensified at Tsholotsho and Domboshawa to instil into the Africans the Alvord recommendations. However, as years went by, the newly trained African demonstrators came into conflict with the locals. On one hand, the white settlers needed labourers to work in the mines and farms, on the other, the local people refused because they could succeed without working for settlers. But dispossession of land and increase of tax made life unbearable. Still the people managed to resist for a while.

In 1947, the first African Secondary School run by government named Goromonzi was opened. Prior to that virtually the Africans were left at the mercy of the missionaries who constructed schools, hospitals and clinics. The Colonial Government wanted cheap labour from students who failed to qualify to enrol at Goromonzi School. Education came as an accident and was considered an act of benevolence by Europeans to civilize those "hewers of wood and drawers of water" as far as Europeans were concerned. This made life very difficult for the African people who struggled up hill with very little resources. This is another type of economic violence as well. It can also be termed violence in education.

There are so many reasons why indigenous Zimbabweans took up arms to wage an armed struggle against the powerful colonial military machine. Chief among these, was the land issue which became the battle cry of 'mwanawevhu' (son of the soil) because the African people realized that in the 1960s, 90% of them depended on the land of which they had been dispossessed. Added to this, in the cities and towns, Africans were not regarded as permanent residents at all. Residing in urban areas was always on temporary basis. By 1925, recognition came that the Africans needed permanent residence in the cities. It was never fulfilled. Why? This was not achieved because Africans were given very limited accommodation as they were supposed to stay in the rural areas, in their impoverished rural homes. The land was very little in fact, the land was being depleted because of the population growth. The little land which was assigned to the African people was the same land for cultivation and livestock grazing. The colonial government was always accusing Africans of having too many cattle. To solve the problem of landlessness, the Rhodesian government introduced de-stocking. The Africans resisted. It was the question of land which had been robbed from them that led to their abject poverty, subjugation and suffering.

Africans were instructed to have a limited number of cattle which they referred to as 'nhimura', (in English they call it destocking). Africans lost many animals especially cattle and goats because any excess number beyond the prescribed limit were taken away by the white farmers for a song. Whites wanted to ensure that Africans would remain doing the manual labour as non-skilled or semi-skilled people. Depriving Africans of their cattle was the worst kind of humiliation to the locals but it was nothing compared with that caused by the seizure of livestock in order to extract hut tax.

Hut tax had to be paid in cash. The settlers strongly believed that this would force African men to work for prolonged periods at low wages. However, tax was also paid in the form of grain and livestock. Surprisingly, whites deliberately kept the prices of these commodities extremely low in order to force men to go and work on the white farms, plantations and mines. In farming, the settlers realized that by the 1930s, Africans were now producing 2.5 million bags of maize annually for their own use and for sale. The settler state then responded by introducing the Maize Control Act in 1931 which was later amended in 1934. This was a deliberate effort to favour settler farmers at the expense of local farming (often scorned at as 'kaffir – farming') and to force the locals to seek employment as cheap labourers on the white farms and mines, where they earned slave wages.

It is therefore indisputable that the settlers used violence in order to force the locals to work on their farms and mines. The colonial police and informal African agents press-ganged the locals into labour through beatings and threats. The situation was worsened by the Master and Servant Ordinance Act of 1901, which made it extremely difficult if not impossible for workers to receive compensation for abuse-related injury. On the contrary, severe penalties were imposed on the workers for the smallest infringements against their employers.

The First Chimurenga

The word, "Chimurenga" means a War of Resistance against foreign occupation in the 1890s and the armed struggle from the 1960s to independence in 1980. In the First Chimurenga, the war was believed to have been led by Murenga, a Shona warrior-ancestor who resisted by any means possible. The word Chimurenga can be used in different contexts. In 1893 as mentioned earlier, the war flared up in Matabeleland mainly because of a clash of cultures after the white settlers tried to control Lobengula's sovereignty over Mashonaland. The rich gold deposits, which the Pioneers hoped to find in Mashonaland did not materialize, so the white settlers turned to farming and in the process dispossessing the local inhabitants off fertile lands.. The Chartered BSA Company and the settlers started looting both the Shona and AmaNdebele properties between October 1893 and early 1896. By March 1896, between 100 000 and 200 000 cattle were seized from the Ndebele people.

According to Ian Phimister, (1988) the settlers knew that this was double tragedy for the Ndebele people. For the African people, cattle were important for food and payment According to Ian Phimister, (1988) the settlers knew that this was double tragedy for the Ndebele people. For the African people, cattle were important for food and payment of bride price. The raiders who invaded Matabeleland were comprised of armed gangs of settlers and reinforced by a contingency of the British South

Africa Company (BSAC) police, who were armed with maximguns. They roamed across the country-side looting whatever they could grab or loot in the process. In some instances the marauding invaders would face stiff resistance from the local people and were even driven off in a concerted show of force.

Whilst such violence ensued, the invasions and occupation of the country were directly affecting the local population. The practices associated with that war had far-lasting consequences on both the black and white generations to come in Rhodesia. The initial premise of this work is that, War and Violence, rather than being confined to their time and space, permeate the normalcy of societal political process.

Local people who refused to reveal where cattle were being hidden would be put to death. In one incident, about four women were shot in cold blood because they refused to reveal where the cattle were. However, raids of this kind missed too many cattle. In 1895 the Company began recruiting the so-called native police with the express intention of making the cattle levies more efficient. The native police then started using some of the local people to advise the local inhabitants to voluntarily hand over their cattle to the authorities. The African police were also to assemble forced labour for the mines and farms.

By November 1895 cattle holdings of the AmaNdebele had been reduced to an estimated 74 000 and yet this area was, traditionally a ranching area. For the next three months they were almost reduced by half again as the BSAC quickened the pace of confisticating cattle. The reason was that the company had realised that once they took natives' cattle then, the white settlers stood to gain by getting the cattle and that the local people would be left with nothing. Indirectly, the psychological effects of the cattle seizures were immense. Cattle signified a lot in the lives of the Shona and AmaNdebele people. Therefore the natives would end up seeking for employment from the invaders and the settlers. This also became one of the causes of the First Chimurenga.

The fighting power and the military strength of the AmaNdebele people was only squashed but not annihilated completely. In 1893, following the death of King Lobengula, Nyamanda one of his elder sons took over as King in June of 1896. On 20th of March 1896, the Ndebele went on strike again against the BSAC and the settlers. One of the causes was rinderpest, (a viral disease that kills cattle) which devastated a large number of cattle in 1896. To contain the spread of the disease, BSAC officials began shooting the cattle that belonged to the AmaNdebele. This was interpreted as extreme provocation by the AmaNdebele people. The early quarantine measures which were meant to save their cattle was regarded with suspicion by the AmaNdebele. They regarded the move as a measure to totally eliminate their cattle. Certainly, general awareness of the intolerability of the existing situation at length, was exacerbated by that natural disaster. Thus on the 20th of March 1896 the Chimurenga war broke out.

When the Shona people heard the news of the uprising and the confrontational attitude of the intruders, the situation was exacerbated. This made the Shona people to revolt, especially due to what they had gone through in the last six years under BSAC occupation. Others successfully resisted the company's administrative pretensions, the ever rising taxes and labour demands.

For example in the then Salisbury District, Kunzvi Nyandoro's people refused to bow before the BSAC by shooting tax collectors in October 1895 and by threatening to kill all police and whites in their district in April 1896.

Up north, the Shona people heard news and the defiant attitude of the intruders. The Shona were preparing not only to revolt, but also to launch a full scale war against the maraudinginvaders. However, in the vast region stretching far to the North and East of Mupfure River, local people were inspired by the spirit medium of Sekuru Kaguvi and Mbuya Nehanda the Mhondoro (*Shona Spirit Medium*) and they quickly joined in the fighting. In other parts of the country, such as the Southern side the chieftainships of Gutu, Zimuto, Chirimumhanzu, Mativi and Chivi, who used to occasionally fight with the Ndebele, preferred to remain neutral and in some cases they were indifferent to the war effort. Perhaps they feared their neutrality would be judged between the Ndebele and the BSAC strength. As a result, the BSAC, with the help of the imperial forces was able to concentrate its strength on some of the selected Shona rulers who resisted them.

A classical example is that of Chief Makoni in the Manicaland area who was defeated and executed in August 1896. It is clear even from oral history that Makoni became a target of the invading forces because he had succeeded in rooting out many of the Pioneers to the extent that word came from the Queen to say she wanted to get hold of Makoni to behead him in London. That was proof that Makoni had exhibited valour against the Pioneer forces. To date, the head of Makoni is believed to be still in London.

Executions without trial were frequent and arson on the villages became a burning passion. Despite the series of Indabas (dialogues) from August to October between the Amandebele and Cecil John Rhodes, most of the indabas failed and the fighting continued especially in Mashonaland region and this resistance persisted right up to 1897. The First Chimurenga war was a sign that the local people could not accept the white man's rule without putting up fierce resistance. The local people went down fighting although originally it had not been their intention to fight. It was due to extreme provocation by those-pioneers. In military terms, the local people were vanquished, but in spirit and will power, they were not defeated as we shall see later on in the Second Chimurenga.

URBANISATION, INDUSTRIALISATION AND RACIAL DISCRIMINATION

This Chapter focuses on urbanisation and industrialisation of Zimbabwe between 1900-1945. It covers forced labour which in Shona is known as 'chibharo' and then poll tax or hut tax. It was evident that urbanization and racism constituted institutionalized violence. There is also the matter of shops owned by black traders which the colonialists referred to as "*Kaffir Shops*". In the final analysis human labour can be very rewarding and, dignifying but forced labour is pure and unmistakable slavery.

According to historical evidence, Provincial Labour Bureaus were formed in colonial Rhodesia along some central compounds especially in Bulawayo and in Salisbury. The Labour Board of Southern Rhodesia was established again in the two provincial areas. The Labour Board proved so successful that by 1899 over 600 000 workers were forced to work on mines in Matabeleland.

Of interest was the volume of labour that came from the native department. During the period 1898 -1899 the source of produce market which was open to the black agriculturalists was restricted by some of the larger companies who decided to start importing food supplies from South Africa. This was in order to discourage local people from producing enough food, so that they would end up in despair facing starvation in order for men to volunteer as cheap labour on white farms and mines.

In order to mobilize a huge contingence of forced labour, railway transport was essential, especially the rail link between South Africa and Southern Rhodesia. The so called northern line, which was coming to Bulawayo from Mafeking, the last four hundred miles were pushed at a day, sometimes with very little food to feed the African workers. This railway line was opened in Bulawayo in November of 1897.

Umtali (now Mutare) was linked to the east coast a year later.

At the end of 1902, Salisbury was connected to the railway system. By 1910, Southern Rhodesia was struggling to be a flourishing commercial concern principally for the Chartered Company. As stated earlier, the Company had been given the authority to rule by the British under the auspices of the Royal Charter.

Ian Phimister (1974) states that the living conditions in the compounds were so appalling that the blacks were living in prisonlike conditions. Phimister continues to give the type of mining compound, life style and working conditions, brutality and violence in these compounds, He states that

"Underground workers who had failed to complete their tasks did have their days forfeited but were assaulted on in the spot. On average flogging varied between six and twenty five lashes". (Phimister, I, 1974).

On reading such shocking narration, one realizes that violation of human rights and excessive use of brutality and violence upon the indigenous people by the settlers had long term effects upon generations yet to be born. Africans were just used as labour commodity. "Natives" were treated worse than horses and oxen in so far as labour and profit were concerned. But they could not suffer in silence forever; neither could they remain docile victims.

It is common knowledge among local African people that throughout the 1930s and 1940s, the African in Southern Rhodesia suffered perpetual segregation that they were subjected to by successive colonial governments. This is what was meant by constitutionalised violation and violence. Much as Zimbabweans were renowned for their peaceful nature and politeness, this was misinterpreted for cowardice and fear of the white man. The African had to keep his head down because he would have been pushed off anywhere, even from the side walk. Africans were not even allowed to walk on streets especially on the pavements, even though the Africans were the ones responsible for cleaning both the pavements and the streets.

Housing Woes

As already mentioned, Africans in the then Salisbury and other urban centers like Bulawayo, were denied permanent residence; They could work but they were not allowed to own residential properties. Their place, as Africans was the native reserves. The contradiction was that the same land which the African was expected to depend on, had been seized by the same settlers who denied Africans ownership of property in urban areas.

The issue of Africans having no permanent accommodation or housing in the urban areas was exacerbated by the growing numbers of workers without accommodation. Finally, the colonial government found it not only necessary to construct houses but also imperative. Most African labourers could only be visited by their families in towns under very strict conditions. This was humiliating for both the visitors and hosts.

Another humiliating experiences was the frequent inspections in the houses to make sure that the Africans could not have relatives visiting them. Urban workers had to seek permission for any relative who visited them for a limited period. This continued up to 1974. The random and violent inspections from the police took place at anytime of the night as oppressive authorities preferred. It was a pathetically degrading experience that kept reminding the Africans that they really did not belong to the city, but to the rural areas. To add insult to injury, the rural soils were arid and infertile. The infrastructure in rural areas was not developed in terms of road network, whilst schools and clinics were few and far between. Those that were operating were being run by missionaries.

The white population had certainly lost its head right from the moment they were allowed to govern themselves. What they forgot was that they were presiding over a disgruntled African populace. A volcano was slowly smouldering in the minds of the local people. Whites did not realize that those seemingly timid people would rise and wage a revolutionary war against white domination. That is what took place during the Second Chimurenga War.

Accumulative testimonies on the effects of oppression and repression from one generation to another, was a source of inspiration for the Africans in colonial Rhodesia. The Africans could not continue to suffer anymore because their human dignity was being violated. Their way of life was disturbed and destroyed in many ways. Families were, to a large extent, separated. Those who came to seek jobs in the cities left behind families at their rural homes. Sometimes married couples did not stay together for long periods ranging from one year to two years, depending on the distance where the head of the family was working.

Getting a professional job or skilled jobs was not easy for Africans. They were only expected to be cheap labourers on farms, mines and as domestic hands. The Africans were never expected to do any white collar jobs. Colour-bar or racial discrimination ensured that Africans could not be employed in policy making positions as managers, or administrators. Worse still, their wages were very low. Whether an African was qualified academically did not matter as most jobs were reserved for Europeans only. There were so many jobs which some whites were unqualified to perform academically, but because of the colour of their skins, they stood a better chance to be employed.

Job reservations caused a lot of suffering and psychological torture to non whites. Such privileges that were reserved for whites only gave them an air of superiority. Chances of promotion at work places for Africans were next to nothing. If one was an African it required a long time for one's potential to be fully realised. Racial discrimination at work places was rampant, to the extend that even educated African workers were not allowed to use the same toilets and cafeteria as their white counterparts.

There were many typical cases of discrimination right up to independence in 1980. At Silveira House in Harare for example, during civic workshops, some of the African participants were complaining about racial prejudice. The Workshop Conveners used to advise the Africans who did vehicle repairs to continue performing their duties because one day opportunities would come their way. After independence the so called unskilled African "*spanner boy*" only needed to study the theoretical side of mechanics to become a fully fledged artisan.

Course conveners offered such advice because there was no other alternative. The most painful part of course was that the African could dismantle the whole engine, repaired it, and reassemble the engine, without the assistance of the white boss, but the African was not allowed to start the engine! The white man would then go to start the vehicles then report that he had finished the work. He would keep the keys and when the owner came, the white man was the one who signed the job card when the work had been done by an African. Neither credit nor recognition was accorded to the African who had actually done the job.

When it came to remuneration, the African was paid spannerboy or non skilled labourer's wages which was peanuts. But the very white man from the time of recruitment would go through the initial training under tutelage from the same spanner boy. At the end of the week, the white man received a salary which was five times more than the African who trained the white man.

Another painful episode happened is during the war of liberation. Three quarters of the armed forces in Rhodesian Security Forces (RSF) were black. The anti-guerrilla campaign was taking its toll among whites in Rhodesia, in terms of manpower and cost of the war. By 1977, at least 47 percent of the country's revenue went to the war effort and the government was forced to recruit more blacks to fight against their brothers and sisters in the nationalist guerrilla forces. From the smallest military unit to the largest, the officer corps were whites, and infantry troops were black. The black soldiers were ordered to fight against the freedom fighters that were liberating the country.

The same happened to blacks in the police force. Until 1974, there was not a single African in the police force who held the post of sergeant until the first five blacks were passed out to take such responsibilities in 1976. Yet four out of five members of the police force were blacks. Only one fifth of the white police force took all the senior officers' posts. Most of the people whom they arrested and cases they had to follow through were done by black people. As a result, this caused a lot of resentment and bitterness among the African people.

In hospitals if a black person got injured, an ambulance reserved for Africans was dispatched. If an ambulance reserved for Europeans passed by the scene of accident, the injured African was left behind. Equally, an ambulance reserved for blacks would leave behind an injured European until the ambulance for Europeans was called in to pick up the patient. One example

is that of the brother of Ms Fay Chung, a former Minister of Education in the government of independent Zimbabwe. The brother
got injured in a road traffic accident and an ambulance was
sent. When the driver saw the injured person whom he had
mistaken for a white man and then realized he was of Asian
origin, a driver for coloured people had to be called in pick up
the patient. Mr. Chung could have died because he was of the
'wrong colour'. When the ambulances first arrived, Chung was
bleeding. This is another example of institutionalised and constitutionalised violation.

In the mind of the colonialist, an African was paid to work
and not to think. Racism and apartheid were a constitutional
right for every Rhodesian city and town such as Salisbury and
Bulawayo. Africans were not allowed to buy in the same shops
as Europeans until 1977. For Africans, there were some windows
reserved where they were served. In hotels or restaurants, Africans
would use a pigeon hole where food would be served to them
because they were not allowed to sit on tables inside the hotel.
There were no places where Africans could sit and eat, even
though the Africans could be the waiters and the cooks.

VIOLATION OF PRIVACY IN URBAN AREAS

Violation of privacy and deprivation in urban areas was also rampant in colonial Rhodesia. The author vividly remembers blacks residing in the then National Township (now Mbare) in the then City of Salisbury (now Harare) The authorities allowed the police to march into the African hostels in order to flush out extra people staying without permits. There was pandemonium! Some youths designed resistance strategies as a response to what they perceived as unwarranted invasion to their privacy. The delegations representing the inhabitants tried to meet the police and explain why they should be allowed to accommodate some extra people on a temporary basis. Their grievance, among a lot others, was that they could not get adequate accommodation anywhere in the city as there were no new houses being built in the African Townships. The housing waiting list was long and was taking too long to clear. Sometimes it took more than ten years for a worker to be allocated a house or flat.

The police were arrogant and hostile. They refused to listen to the grievances. In the end, the people took the law into their hands resulting in ugly skirmishes. Police quickly called in reinforcement from the Army around midnight. The army unit arrived and the hostel dwellers went to meet the commanders and explained what had transpired. The army unit understood the situation and agreed that the housing issue was critical and needed to be given due attention. The Army unit sought dialogue with the policemen who had caused havoc. The army told the police that they were causing violence in towns yet the war of liberation was ragging. The army officers warned the police to stop raiding the hostels. This was a clear case of the police displaying poor mob control and the Army was quick to understand civil military relations.

During the same period, the colonial government came out with a scheme to lure one million Europeans to come and settle in the country. Those immigrants were to be given citizen status and live in the country forever. A housing scheme was icing sugar to attract the new settlers. Money was promised to the white immigrants for them to start a new life. Yet there was no money to provide accommodation for the African people who were already working. There was not enough money to train Africans who were citizens by birth. On the contrary, the colonial regime had enough money to spend on one million new immigrants, who had to be white so that they would increase the number of Europeans to be settled in Rhodesia.

On the other hand, one should appreciate the background and environment in which Robert Mugabe and Joshua Nkomo grew up in, at a time when the First Chimurenga was still vividly remembered. Most of the people who had survived the First Chimurenga, were still much alive and narrated tales of what had happened. The entrenched white political, economic, social and cultural structures could only be broken by a counter force of firm black resistance. Furthermore, the 1923 Constitution had aroused emotions and anger among the Africans. In order to qualify to vote and to participate in the parliamentary processes, one had to have a minimum of $150 worth of property and an income of at least $100 a year. Another option was to register a mining claim or to have attained a certain minimum standard of academic education.

Adult whites met those requirements but virtually all adult blacks did not possess them. Even though the population at the time in 1923 was estimated at around 900 000 blacks in Southern Rhodesia, they were only 34 000 whites in the country and a small minority from Asia. The reason of bringing this issue is to show how slim chances were for Africans to participate directly in politics on an equal footing as citizens living in the same country.

When the Industrial Action which took place in 1947 led by Benjamin Burombo is reviewed, it clearly shows that it was driven by desperation, because the people had suffered so much. It has to be acknowledged that such an industrial action had to be undertaken by people who had decided between life and death at that point in time as there was not a single African political party which was allowed to operate freely in the country.

It was then very difficult for Africans to participate in national politics. The uprising of blacks in the First Chimurenga had taught whites not to take chances with the local people. Africans had no say in the running of the country. Decisions about the welfare of African people were taken by whites and their future was determined for them by the white rulers.

Earlier on we discussed about the need for cheap labour which was needed by the settlers and also by the BSAC. Eventually, forced labour was introduced in Southern Rhodesia. According to Ian Phimister (1988) there is enough evidence that, between 1900 and1950, at least 35,000 Africans died in the mines. The causes of the deaths were attributed to long hours of work, very poor food, very dangerous working conditions. Very little attention was paid to health matters and as a result, such a large number of Africans died.

The Emergence of a New Generation of African Resistance

Most political parties were started among the Africans long after the Second World War (1939-1945). However some strong political voices started to be heard after that war. Joshua Nkomo, a social worker and trade unionist, was invited to participate in the conference that was crafting the Federation of Rhodesia and Nyasaland in 1952 in which the black delegates to the conference were unanimous in their call for freedom. However, the political atmosphere on the ground in 1952 was not ripe for African political parties. People needed to be educated, mobilised and assisted for them to understand what political parties were for.

The industrial action which was led by Benjamin Burombo in 1974 gave some ray of hope to many young African people especially those who were getting more education. Africans had to realise also that many young men who wanted to further their education went down to the Union of South Africa. Those who were educated there later became popular political leaders; the likes of Robert Mugabe, Joshua Nkomo, Josiah Chinamano, Simon Muzenda, Maurice Nyagumbo and many others who were prepared to come together and make a meaningful political contribution. That was how the City Youth was formed by James Chikerema, George Nyandoro, Edson Sithole and Dunduza Chisiza in 1957.With the advent of these men, early movements of non tribal associations and protest lost momentum. This changed the tempo from years of passive protest to the period of resistance which had begun in earnest.

The Youth League was a group of educated young blacks who were frustrated by the older generation of Africans who appeared too scared to neither confront the regime head-on nor give the new generation of young political activists in the City

League political space to manoeuvre. The new leaders were branded hooligans or a bunch of violent people. The whites forgot that these were young men who were - ghting for a just cause – their freedom.

The likes of James Chikerema, George Nyandoro and others, were some of the leaders who did a sterling job in trying to organize the Youth League. This was after they had realized that without involvement in politics, there was no future for the Africans living in colonial Rhodesia, especially with dissenting strong voices like those of Ian Smith. In 1951, Smith was quoted in parliament saying, the vote of the uneducated African would hold as much weight as the vote of the most skilled and the most civilised European.

From the foregoing, one could discern that educated African young men were targeted for persecution by people like Ian Smith. That is why the Africans launched the City Youth League after realizing that time was running out. Some whites were also aware that young African men who were working and breaking their backs for meagre wages were becoming politically restless.

Black miners supplemented their rations which they bought from the local store, by visiting nearby villages to buy food and also by hunting and - shing as they were earning very little money. They did not have enough food. Such experiences resulted in the emergence of a new generation of African leaders who were attracted to the resistance movement against white oppression.

Poor diet and squalid living conditions led to a high mortality rate among African labourers. Conservative estimates of pneumonia and scurvy, and to a less extent tuberculosis, dysentery, in- uenza and syphilis, altogether claimed the lives of about 34 000 black miners between 1900 and 1950. Some of these young men whom Ian Smith said were backward and useless knew what was happening. That is why there was the industrial action in 1947 led by Benjamin Burombo. Because of poor working conditions, their fellow brothers had perished. In the Mining Industry for instance, pneumonia, which was rampant at that time, could have been prevented by warm clothing, decent housing and proper feeding. Indeed long hours and low wages were the basis of rapid expansion of the mining industry after 1903.

Black workers were paid, not by calendar month, but only on the completion of a ticket which was divided into thirty working days. This meant that it could take anything between 35 to 45 days to complete a ticket. Unless workers took matters into their own hands, there would not be any respect for their rights.

Before 1914, compulsory days of rest were unheard of in the mines and on the farms. After the pronouncement of compulsory days of rest the law was usually ignored by those ruthless employers. The question to ask is who were the backward people between the whites and blacks? That was certainly violence perpetrated by the people who claimed to be Christians and civilized.

THE RISE OF AFRICAN NATIONALISM

After the success of the Youth League in 1957, the Southern Rhodesia African National Congress (ANC) was formed in 1958. The government of Edgar Whitehead banned the ANC and on 29 February 1959, the National Democratic Party (NDP) led by Joshua Nkomo immediately replaced it. Scores of people who were alleged to have been involved in the formation and leadership of these parties were arrested. Their activities were seen as subversive by the colonial government.

Towards the end of 1960, representatives of major white political parties were involved in talks in London concerning Southern Rhodesia. In February 1961 Whitehead and the British colonial Secretary Don Kensadish signed agreed proposals for a new constitution.

Under the constitutional proposals, the Southern Rhodesian Parliament seats would be increased to sixty five. Of these, 50 could be elected by the highly qualified citizens. The other 15 would be elected by those with lower qualifications. Such qualifications were based on education, income and property ownership. Because of the structures that were based on racial discrimination, very few blacks would qualify. This was a deliberate attempt to discourage the black voters. The development incensed the young African nationalists especially those who had travelled abroad and on the African continent and tasted freedom.

The battle cry and slogan of the nationalists was "*One Person One Vote*". This was because of the discriminatory for voting qualifications imposed by the white regime to stifle Africans from voting. The banned ANC, which had been revived in January 1960 as the NDP, intensified the call for "*One Man*

One Vote". In that turbulent atmosphere, Ian Smith, being one of the right wingers, decided to form a new political party for whites, the Rhodesian Front (RF). The RF manifesto was adamant that as a party it did not believe in universal suffrage.

In December of 1961, Ian Smith held his inaugural congress. The aim of the congress was to woo more white supporters. While Smith was doing that, Sir Edgar Whitehead banned the NDP. Joshua Nkomo and Reverend Ndabaningi Sithole retaliated within eight days by forming the Zimbabwe African People's Union (ZAPU). The objective of ZAPU was to establish a more radical and stronger nationalist party. They realized that the African people were not being given the democratic space which they had long agitated for, yet the whites were entrenching themselves in power.

The Rhodesian Front (RF)

When the whites realised that ZAPU was becoming more and more radical, Ian Smith formed a more extremist right wing Rhodesian Front to counter the nationalist movement. This came about because the Rhodesians, including Ian Smith, condemned Edgar Whitehead's government with accusations accepting the possibility of a handover of power to the blacks.

The third voice besides that of ZAPU and the RF was that of Sir Garfield Todd, who had been Prime Minister before. Todd opposed the 1961 constitution. He told the Committee that the Declaration of Rights contained in the "new constitution" was being given to the people as a substitute for the vote. On consideration alone, it was quite useless therefore and not acceptable to the African people who constituted 92% of the population. The constitution did not give any protection against repressive laws.

Comparatively speaking, and listening to those three voices, one could read that a fierce confrontation was building up, and tensions were rising high.

In 1962, the Catholic Bishop's Conference gave a very strong warning through the Catholic Magazine, Motto, stating that if the racial tensions continued, the Catholic Bishops could foresee a civil war in the country in the next five years. And they were right. That is when the 1961 Constitution became law, worsening an already turbulent situation. The whites were divided, whilst the blacks were very clear in their rejection of the 1961 Constitution. Some flimsy courtesy campaign was called by the white liberals in order to alleviate some racial ill feelings, By so doing they believed it was possible to persuade black people to register as voters.

ZAPU called for the boycott of the election as more violence ensued. The petrol bomb was the weapon of choice that was used and was targeting houses and properties of those blacks who were sympathetic to the prevailing political climate. On August 20th 1962, ZAPU was banned and a number of its leading figures were all detained. Nkomo and Ndabaningi Sithole were at that time outside the country. When Nkomo returned in October he was restricted. Reverend Ndabaningi Sithole stayed in Tanzania and immediately formed the Zimbabwe African National Union (ZANU).

After the formation of ZANU, there were a lot of skirmishes and fighting between ZAPU and ZANU supporters, across the whole country especially in the African townships. The violence spread into the rural areas claiming a number of lives. Civic leadership was unheard of at that time neither was training for leadership. Therefore, people had to express their frustrations through violence. This then became the root cause of the violence which erupted between the two parties ZANU and ZAPU at independence in 1980, and thereafter.

Violation and violence continued for some time. Churches were burnt down and property was destroyed. Some nationalists decided to embark on acts of sabotage targeting economic infrastructure and some Africans whom they believed were collaborating with the whites. For example, nationalist resistance leaders went on a rampage attacking some farms belonging to whites, cutting down tobacco and green mealies during the night.

In the meantime, RF was fogging ahead galvanizing support within the white community. Meanwhile, Winston Field became Prime Minister winning a parliamentary majority of just five; this included Ian Douglas Smith who was retained in his Umzingwane constituency. Smith was appointed as Deputy Prime Minister and Minister of Finance. Field also tried to implement some cosmetic improvements in race relations in his new Government by freeing the African nationalists, who had been incarcerated before the elections.

Field freed the detainees in January 1963 and urged them to work within the system. At first he thought it was going to work. The nationalists were decisive and they made it clear that they would rather work with the RF, whose policies were not misunderstood, because they were frank. In other words, the nationalists knew who the enemy was. To them, the RF was a more easily identifiable enemy than Field. The white supremacists were hardening up and Winston Field; the Prime Minister had to resign, because he could not pacify the Rhodesian whites.

The Emergence of Ian Douglas Smith and the Coming of UDI

In the last chapter we saw how Winston Field failed to contain white attitudes towards black resistance. In these circumstances Ian Douglas Smith saw himself as the embodiment of the old imperial Europe with its supremacist virtues. He was unable to distinguish between "actual" and "factual". A Hurricane fighter pilot during the Second World War, Smith took power in 1964 at the age of forty-five. According to Matthew C. White the RF precisely had been formed from the basis of preventing the handover of power to blacks. Secondly, the RF party was certainly not going to accept wider franchise for local blacks. Now firmly in power, Smith was going to put his word into practice.

Smith's first act as Prime Minister, was obviously directed against the black nationalists. He had enough reason to clamp down on the African groups because of the political violence that had flared up, following the split between ZAPU and ZANU in August of 1963. Robert Mugabe, among other leaders, went along with Reverend Ndabaningi Sithole to form ZANU. Joshua Nkomo on the other hand, also established a People's Caretaker Council, (PCC) as an arm of the banned ZAPU.Those who lived between 1963 and 1964 can recall very well the amount of violence that escalated between the blacks who sided with either party. At the same time the black nationalists realized that the hard-core Rhodesians were not going to waste their time talking to black nationalists. Both sides were affected by the laager mentality. Whites were going to be vicious by using the strong arms of Government, notwithstanding the threat they faced. Their policy was so brutal and so was the war. Blacks also realized that, they too had to react using agitation and civil disobedience to get their freedom. They were, as it later emerged, in for a rude awakening for failing to analyse their different circumstances, compared to the situation that had prevailed in Nyasaland and Northern Rhodesia.

The first acts of sabotage were recorded during that period. Consequently, within a couple of weeks, after Ian Smith took office, he clamped down on the PCC and ZANU leadership inside Rhodesia. The period after the assumption of power by Ian Smith led to threats of arrests and reprisals on many African political activists. These threats arose from the fact that blacks found themselves embedded in a human environment which generated extreme and unbearable social, economic and political pressures.

The threats manifested themselves in a number of ways. The four basic types were physical threats (pain, death and injury) economic threats (seizure or destruction of property, denial of access to work or resources) and threats to civil liberties (imprisonment). Joshua Nkomo who was the leader of ZAPU was restricted to Gonakudzingwa together with some of his colleagues. It will be recalled that many families suffered after their fathers had been detained or restricted. The whites were hardening up and so was the resolve of the nationalists. This erased any room for dialogue or negotiations. Certainly, from the mounting human rights violations, there was increased resistance among blacks in return.

In order to have some Africans rubber stamping his political motives, Ian Smith tactically gathered over 622 of the 810 recognized African leaders, for a conference to approve his rise to power. The press was barred from covering the proceedings. Ian Smith himself was present. The chiefs reportedly agreed to accept what had happened and were urged to support Ian Smith's stance on the Unilateral Declaration of Independence (UDI). They called it "our independence", but in actual fact it meant European or white Rhodesian independence. At that meeting, the response of the invited chiefs was recorded as "unanimous support for independence". Smith also went on and sought similar backing from the white electorate, which, on 5 November 1964, was recorded as overwhelming thus endorsing Smith as the leader of Rhodesia.

In the meantime, on the African nationalist front, both ZAPU and ZANU had made a solemn decision that the armed struggle was the only option left to final victory for the African people.

THE ARMED STRUGGLE: CHIMURENGA II

The armed struggle to liberate Zimbabwe was launched from two different fronts and by two different liberation movements, namely the Zimbabwe People's Revolutionary Army (ZIPRA) which was the armed wing of ZAPU and the Zimbabwe African National Liberation Army, the armed wing of ZANU. ZIPRA's rear base was in Zambia whilst that of ZANLA was in Mozambique. The armed struggle was mooted in the 1960s, primarily as urban forms of protest against an increasingly oppressive white regime.

The Rhodesian police had crushed the protests physically, but as mentioned earlier on, the will to resist by the Africans remained. No matter how many people were jailed, injured or killed, the Africans were determined to fight on. This radicalized other nationalists, who began to consider an armed resistance as the last option. The "land issue" also became the rallying point. It became the underlying reason for the war. An estimated 60 000 people of all races (but mainly Africans) lost their lives, about 200 000 were injured and half the nation were left suffering from Post Traumatic Stress Disorder (PTSD) because of the war. (Rupiya, M, unpublished seminar paper, 1999)

The largest number of casualties was the rural poor. The rural areas were easily to penetrate by the guerrillas since they could get their provisions in terms of food, recruits, intelligence and clothing without detection by the RSF. Consequently, the rural areas became the battlefield (operational theatre of war) where violence took its toll in the form of whippings, beatings, rape, torture, murder and mayhem. The violence upon the peasants was mainly perpetrated by the RSF, the police and to some extent by the ZANLA and ZIPRA guerrillas.

Women Bear the Brunt of the War

Women bore the brunt of war. An increasingly common feature of the war was sexual violence. Women and girls were the main victims and subjected to rape and sexual slavery. Sexual violence against women was used as a means to humiliate, intimidate and demoralise both African men and women who were supporting the guerrillas. Women were raped in full view of their families as a way to force them to dishonour their allegiance to freedom fighters, their communities and also to humiliate or demoralize their men. Such atrocities destroyed community and family cohesion. It had both emotional and physical effects which were very devastating. Effects included physical and emotional trauma, sexually transmitted infections, unwanted pregnancies and sometimes permanent harm to reproductive health. In other communities, the rape victims were ostracised by their husbands, societies and families.

A key feature of this situation was the total impunity with which the crimes were committed. The raped victims were prevented from seeking justice because of fear, embarrassment and a sense of hopelessness and also they could not afford to access the legal system. This created a situation where violence against women was seen as routine, rather than criminal.

Besides rape, women could not runaway and leave their children behind when a village was attacked. Neither could they run away and leave the elderly or the sick whom they were looking after. Pregnancy itself became a death warrant. Guerrillas and the RSF were suspicious of who had impregnated the women. In the end, the poor woman would be killed on suspicion that either side had made her pregnant.

Guerrilla tactics implied that the freedom fighters had to disguise themselves largely as ordinary or lay people. They had to pretend to be ordinary people in order to take the enemy by surprise, and disappear into the dark or disappear into the crowds. By so doing, the guerrillas needed the unwavering support from ordinary people.

The methods of recruitment for both liberation movements were very taxing. In Zambia, by 1971 the Zambian Government had put some restrictions or conditions on the method of recruitment by both ZAPU and ZANU on its soil. This was mainly because Zimbabweans, who were working in Zambia by then, were pressganged into joining the liberation war. Some of those recruits left behind wives and children without any support or means of survival. The young men ended up joining the armed struggle and many of them did not make it as they perished in the struggle. Since the two armed liberation movements could not continue to force people to join them, they had to recruit lots of young men and women, especially from 1973 onwards. However, the majority of young men and women who joined the armed struggle did so through persuasion rather than coercion.

The guerrillas received only basic military training. In the beginning, they were trained for six months but by the time the war ended, guerrilla recruits were trained for only three months to flood the battle field with armed fighters. After training, guerrillas were allocated weapons of war and deployed into the front. The villagers or "povo" continued supplying food, clothing, medicines and also intelligence to guerrillas.

Some specialized guerrilla units received further tactical training in countries overseas and in Africa. For example, the ZANLA forces who attacked the national oil depot in the middle of Salisbury on 12 December, 1978 displayed a high level of military training. There was also the shooting down of two Viscount Aircrafts at Victoria Falls and Kariba when the guerrillas used heat-seeking missiles.

Such sophistication mounted pressure for a political settlement which led to internal negotiations between Ian Smith, Bishop Muzorewa, the Reverend Ndabaningi Sithole and Chief Jeremiah Chirau.

Security for freedom fighters depended upon the ordinary people. Therefore, guerrillas had to convince the ordinary population first that liberation would only come through the "barrel of a gun". They had to explain to the ordinary people on their mission and then convince them that they were fighting against an oppressive regime. To win the hearts and minds of the local populace guerrilla forces had to use persuasion where it worked. Where persuasion failed guerrilla forces had to apply force. Persuasion was usually very successful where people had not experienced the nasty consequences of reprisals from the RSF for supporting guerrillas. Guerrillas were regarded by the Rhodesian authorities as "terrorists" or criminals. The punishment metered out to rural villagers for supporting or hiding "terrorists" was death. In many cases civilians were imprisoned or executed as terrorists or terrorist collaborators who had failed to report the presence of terrorist, which was in itself a very serious offence.

It is believed that the first guerrilla forces who came back into Zimbabwe to fight, did not find it easy. Such guerrillas operated in Matabeleland North with the help of "Umkonto Wesizwe" (MKK), the military wing of the African National Congress of South Africa. The joint MKK/ZIPRA guerrilla operations drew in the South Africa Police (SAP) and later the South African Defence Force (SADF) into the war supporting the Rhodesians war.

The ZIPRA guerrilla forces faced a number of challenges which included rough terrain, oppressive heat; lack of contact with the peasantry and of cause, the mighty Zambezi River which they had to cross without being spotted by the RSF or attacked by crocodiles and hippos. They were learning for the first time how to engage the enemy.

This brings us to the first pitched battle between the RSF and the ZANLA guerrilla forces. This battle came to be known as the Chinhoyi Battle. The freedom fighters decided to engage the enemy face to face. The young freedom fighters fought tenaciously a pitched battle that lasted seven hours before they ran out of ammunition. They were all killed. It is undeniable the Zanla freedom fighters put up a brilliant fight, but alas they were still novices in military strategy. They were engaging a conventionally trained army with a sophisticated back up system of manpower, ground force supported by the Air Force. On the guerrilla side, they had very limited weaponry which they had to carry on their backs all the way from Zambia, across the mighty Zambezi River to the combat zones. The freedom fighters did not have a clear logistical system of re-supply of food, weaponry and munitions. Guerrillas had to learn war strategy and tactics the hard way, but nevertheless the Battle of Chinhoyi will be remembered in the history of Zimbabwe as the turning point in the liberation struggle. After the Chinhoyi Battle, guerrilla training intensified and more rear bases were opened in Mozambique and Zambia spreading as far as Tanzania and Angola.

However, the defeat at Chinhoyi did not dampen the morale of freedom fighters. Instead, new operational frontiers were opened on a wider scale. Nationalist freedom fighters gradually learnt that the guerrilla war was very different, in terms of command, control and communications as compared to conventional warfare. Guerrilla warfare was protracted and brutal because the war had no defined theatre of operation as it has no frontiers. The fighting was sporadic and waged in many places at any given time, involving anybody or everybody, resulting in many casualties.

The Intensification of the Armed Struggle

In 1972 there was the Pierce Commission which was rejected by Africans. As a result, more young men and women decided to join the armed struggle, thus recruitment by both the ZAPU, and ZANU went on smoothly as there was a steady flow of volunteers. In recruiting cadres, in some cases, both persuasive as well as coercive methods were used. By 1972, ZANLA intensified the fighting in the north-east of the country to a point when the Rhodesians realized that the threat was spreading across the whole country. The pattern of the war took the form of assassinations, raids, ambushes, laying of landmines by guerrillas forces, designed to destroy morale among the enemy soldiers and their will to continue fighting.

A number of repressive laws, including the notorious Law and Order (Maintenance Act and the Emergence Powers Act) were then promulgated by the Rhodesian Government. These notorious laws enabled the RSF to carry out violent reprisals against guerrillas and peasants with little fear or legal prosecution.

As the war intensified and the security situation worsened, the RSF increasingly targeted civilians for murder, torture and detention. This was mainly because the RSF "Fire Force" tactical doctrine called the "*body count*" approach where success was measured by the number of corpses brought back after a battle. As guerrilla resistance intensified, the RSF were forced to make up for numbers and increased the body count by killing civilians either in crossfire or shooting them point blank. Just like what the BSAC had done in the First Chimurenga War, the RSF also used the same scotched earth policies to burn down entire villages, shooting or stealing livestock, and destroying growing crops and torching granaries.

Because of the presence of either the RSF or their agents, the mobilisation and politicisation process was usually done with violence and haste. Methods of mobilisation and politicisation were protracted and abrupt. In areas where the guerrillas had no control, they often resorted to abrupt and haphazard mobilisation strategies because they did not have enough time to garner the support of the peasants in such areas, so they resorted to force. Violence was applied to persuade villagers to perform violent acts against each other.

Intensification of the war forced more white people to spend more time in uniform and fighting in operational areas. Not only did the security situation deteriorate, but it was also a drain on the fiscus which adversely affected the economy. The cost of the war to the economy reached one million dollars a day, an astounding figure at that time.

Commercial farming was no longer safe and viable and many farms were vacated because guerrilla forces targeted them. Investor confidence evaporated and the economy nose-dived. As a result, emigration exceeded immigration. The few whites who braved the escalating war spent even more time in uniform. Lieutenant-General Peter Walls, Commander of the Combined Operations concluded that a white military victory is no longer a feasible option as the Zimbabwe's war of liberation had intensified. Both sides began fervent propaganda campaigns to legitimise their course.

During the early days of the liberation struggle, some recruits died in the rear camps. Crossing the border into the front between Zimbabwe and Zambia or between Zimbabwe and Mozambique was also very risky. There are many young men and women who perished while they were crossing the borders to wage the armed struggle in the front. Some were directly shot dead by the

RSF whilst others were caught in crossfire and yet others detonated antipersonnel mines and were blown to smithereens. However, the spirit to join the struggle did not slacken. More and more youths poured out of Rhodesia to join the armed struggle.

During the liberation struggle, new legislation was promulgated to protected Rhodesian uniformed forces from prosecution. Therefore RSF security personnel unleashed violence, killing and maiming civilians knowing fully well that the law would not touch them. Victims could do nothing because the Courts would dismiss the cases as the accused were already indemnified. As stressed earlier, it was, to all intends and purposes, institutionalized violence because the RSF was the security institution in the country. The Indemnity Act was enacted in 1975. There was a clause in it, where the army could apply the scotched earth policy, meaning the Army was destroying food reserves, torch villages and the granaries just to make sure that the guerrillas had nothing to eat. The main aim was to destroy the will of the people not only to exist but to support the guerrillas also.

Morality of Violence through the Struggle

The African nationalists who were directing the war effort against the Rhodesians, namely Nkomo and Mugabe believed that to win a total war through negotiations was not possible and would not be possible. In any case that was not the best option given the stubbornness of the Rhodesian regime. Africans believed that too long a time before final victory was achieved would allow lethargy to creep in among and between their fighting forces thereby making the struggle longer and protracted before Africans could exercise democracy through the ballot box. Victory would only come through the barrel of the gun to give the

Africans an opportunity to choose their own leaders. It became apparent that there was no way the white regime could win the war. Also, it was going to be a mammoth task for the liberation forces to assume power through an outright victory.

The war could have continued unabated but what should be appreciated is that the liberation struggle was a just war, both politically and morally. Morally, because all the other avenues of dialogue, negotiations, strikes and demonstrations had been explored and nothing had been achieved. Dialogue did not work, demonstrations and strikes were crushed. So the only option remaining was to take up arms and wage a protracted armed struggle. That was a difficult choice indeed and a personal sacrifice for those who joined the struggle.

A war is ugly because it is violent. People kill and get killed. Property is destroyed and infrastructure is vandalized, and nothing is left unscathed. There is no progress for individuals and society as a whole.

The RSF quickly learnt guerrilla tactics and strategies. Soldiers started going around the villages promising ordinary people through persuasion that if they saw 'people' dressed in a particular way, armed, looking for food, give them food. If they needed water, they had to be given that water but while they are eating and drinking, the locals should report to the security forces. Once they reported to the security forces, the villagers would be given some money as a reward. However, it turned out not to be a very big reward after all.

On the other side of the coin, if the security forces discovered that a person had been visited by guerrillas forces, fed them, gave them a place to stay, and failed to report their presence to the security forces, that person was arrested. The consequences were that the victim would be imprisoned or otherwise shot on the spot. Indeed, thousands of ordinary people were killed as *"war collaborators who connived with terrorists"*. Thus the ordinary people were caught in the middle because the guerrillas also needed logistical support and food except weaponry.

ZANLA forces were required to apply the Chinese guerrilla philosophy. According to them, the guerrillas were fish in water.

The water represented the peasants and without water, the fish would die. The peasants were regarded as the fountain heads of the revolution. A successful revolution could not be waged without the peasants, because without them, there could be no revolution. And to reject them meant rejecting the revolution. Political mobilisation of the mass of the people became the foundation of winning the war. With a mobilized peasantry in the countryside, ZANLA created a sea of humanity in which the enemy could be swallowed. Violence was regarded as the only means to bring about any social, cultural, economic and political change because negotiations had failed. Freedom fighters were therefore expected to respect the peasants as successful prosecution of the armed struggle depended largely on the local population. To a large extent, that philosophy was accepted as the guiding principle. But sometimes when guerrillas realized they were loosing ground they resorted to apply other coercive tactics.

In 1972 at St Albert's Mission, in the north-east district of Mount Darwin, a group of armed ZANLA forces entered the Mission during the evening. They knew that the whole school would be watching a film and went on to abduct the whole school. Abduction meant forcibly taking people against their will. But this was war and ZANLA needed to recruit more young men and women for guerrilla training if the war was to be won. That was the essence of violation and violence. What has to be realised after taking a person against his or her free will was the arduous task to win the heart and mind of that person to make him or her fight on the side of the freedom fighters. Otherwise they could be engaging people who would be working for the enemy.

The abduction of students and teachers from St Albert was followed by the Rhodesian Army launching a hot pursuit to rescue the abductees. The Rhodesian Forces were fighting to stop the recruits from going for the liberation struggle whilst ZANLA forces were trying to keep going with their new recruits. In such incidents, ordinary people or non-combatants got killed. This was because the would-be recruits did not know how to react under battle conditions. In the fog of battle, some of the students could run towards the Rhodesian soldiers and could get killed, being mistaken for guerrillas or they could run towards the freedom fighters and be mistaken for enemy soldiers. Amid such confusion, many innocent people were killed. The ordinary people had to suffer the consequences from atrocities perpetrated by both sides.

The guerrillas sometimes used coercive tactics and metered out punishment to people suspected of being traitors. At the beginning of the war, the RSF also used psychological warfare and propaganda in an effort to 'win the hearts and minds of the people'. Some ordinary people secretly became agents of the RSF. Such "informers" caused the capture or deaths of many freedom fighters.

Resultantly, the guerrillas forces also embarked on brutal and summary executions of traitors. In other cases when someone was discovered to be an 'informer' of the RSF guerrilla forces executed that person, not only to protect themselves but also as a lesson to like-minded persons. Quite a number of people had their lips cut off, as punishment for having betrayed the struggle, whilst others had their ears and tongues cut off. Such punishment used to deter sell-outs and informers. In the operational areas, sometimes freedom fighters were actually feared by the local populace. If the villagers betrayed freedom fighters or supplied intelligence about the whereabouts of the guerrillas to the RSF, whether willingly or by coercion under torture by RSF, whatever the reason, such people suffered the consequences from the guerrilla forces. Thus some people were killed by guerrillas forces after being accused of being sell-outs or suspected of being informers.

Some local inhabitants voluntarily informed the RSF about the presence of guerrilla forces because they would have gone through the painful experience inflicted upon them by the freedom fighters. If one's mother or any relative had been killed by the guerrillas, in order to avenge, that civilian went and reported the presence of the guerrilla forces in the area. The freedom fighters would then be "flushed out" by the RSF.

In such dicey war games, a culture of violence and counter violence prevailed right across the whole countryside, among and between people, across generations and gender. The result was that people created a new culture of violence which was anathema to the peace loving Zimbabweans.

Even three decades after the liberation struggle had ended, there are many people who have gone through the horror of violation and counter violence. Such people are now adults and some of them occupy influential positions in society. These people are to be found right across the political divide. Some are still active, whilst others are passive in the political arena. All such people have earned for themselves, the culture of violence and violation. Thus vengeance has been with Zimbabwe and will still be part of the society. Violence, in every sphere of life reigns supreme and it is the easiest method to force people to do what the leadership wants. The people of Zimbabwe must understand this reality if the nation is ever to come out of this cycle of violence. Since violence is now in the blood, and a way of life, the million dollar question is what kind of human beings will Zimbabweans be? Vengeance continues unabated engulfing the whole social milieu. However, it is imperative that citizens of Zimbabwe move away from a culture of violence to a culture of peace, reconciliation, forgiveness and national healing.

Protected Villages and Collateral Damage

Protected Villages (PVs) were introduced in 1974 starting in Mashonaland spreading to Manicaland and the Midlands. This was collective punishment on the Africans who supported the armed struggle. Life in the PVs was terrible. Head-bashing and beard-uprooting were the torture methods of choice by armed District Assistants (DAs); later on by the Guard Forces and finally by Bishop Abel Muzorewa's Auxiliary Forces. The villagers could not till their land, attend to their crops or graze their cattle properly as a dusk-to-dawn curfew was introduced. Villagers were only allowed to get out (to their fields and look after cattle) as from six in the morning and made sure they were back in the "keep" by six o'clock in the evening. If anyone broke the curfew they were shot on sight.

The fields of villagers were far away from the "keeps". It was common that cattle and wild animals destroyed the crops. Some of the cattle died after over eating green mealies. This often happened when the PV army commander decided not to allow people to leave the keeps for suspecting them to be ferrying food to feed freedom fighters. Confined for days on end, the cattle would break loose from the pans to find grazing and went straight into the maize fields. That was collective punishment on the humble villagers, who were wondering why they were being punished.

Both the freedom fighters and RSF claimed that they were fighting on behalf of the people. On one hand, the guerrilla claimed they were liberating people from an oppressive system which was being kept in power by the RSF. On the other, the RSF claimed they were liberating people from the communist terrorists. At the end of the day, both sides were causing untold suffering of "the people in the middle". Each side put pressure on the local people to solicit their support (albeit by force). The warring sides needed the support of the populace. But the demands on the villagers went too far when the armed opponents continued punishing the people for supporting either side.

Members of the Catholic Commission for Justice and Peace (CCJP) in Rhodesia carried out a serious investigation and research about the suffering of the ordinary people especially in the rural areas particularly in the traditional war zone. This author was assigned to go to Chiweshe area. The CCJP produced a book called *"The Man in the Middle"* that is the guerrillas on one side, the soldiers on the other and the ordinary people in the middle. In this book the CCJP concluded to take the government to court through the Ministry of Defence. The CCJP sighted the Ministry of Defence to be answerable. The government decided to introduce a bill to protect the Minister of Defence and his colleagues and all members of the RSF especially those that would be on active duty. This resulted in the enactment of the Indemnity Act as mentioned earlier.

In general, the Indemnity Act made some of the ordinary people to be more resolute and committed to the armed struggle because ultimately they realized that their suffering would never come to an end. Therefore it had a boomerang effect.

Sometimes when guerrillas had made successful attacks in the country and then find their way into Mozambique or Zambia, the RSF, would pursue them using another military strategy which they called "Hot Pursuit". The strategy was based upon the RSF deploying security assets which included the Special Air Service Regiment (SAS), Infantry and Armoured Car Units which were available to the RSF and had been inherited in its entirety from the defunct Federal Royal Air force (RAF). Hot Pursuit meant that the RSF would follow the guerrillas right across the borders into neighbouring countries in which they had their bases. Subsequently, the RSF attacked and killed trained guerrillas and innocent refugees in Zambia and Mozambique. A case in point being the massacres by the RSF in holding such as Chimoio, Nyadzonya, Victory and Freedom Camps among others.

Selous Scouts also operated in free zones. They used the style of the guerrillas, such as dressing like guerrillas, talking and simulating guerrilla tactics of looking for food from among the villagers etc. Pretentiously, if they realized that there was a soldier in the area who was on leave, a police officer or government official well known by those villagers, the Selous Scouts would come and capture such a person who would not be aware of their identity. No one would know that they were acting like guerrillas. The pseudo guerrillas would accuse any one they had captured of being a sell-out and torture and kill him in the presence of the ordinary people. Then they would disappear. They would make sure the army would know what had happened. The army would come seeking to revenge the death of their fellow soldier through venting their anger on the unsuspecting villagers. The soldiers would come and shoot at the villagers, destroy their homes by setting them on fire and confiscating their animals. One such incident happened in Musami in which empirical evidence suggested that a group which killed the Musami Missionaries were not guerrillas but that they were members of the Selous Scouts.

Another way of punishing people was through imposing

curfews. Curfew areas varied according to timetables. Some curfew time tables would run from 6pm to 6am the following day but some would go up to 20 hours. The locals would have to look after their cattle, fetch water, go to the fields and do their laundry in two hours. That is impossible for any human being but this happened in Zimbabwe. A 22 hour curfew was introduced in Chiweshe. Periodically the curfew would be 24 hours specially when they had been military engagements between guerrillas and soldiers. The villagers would be told not to move in and out of their villages for the next 24 hours. That meant animals would starve, people would equally not be in a position to get enough food and water to feed themselves.

Schools sometimes had to be closed. In some instances, one could not drink water outside the keeps or outside the consolidated villagers because the RSF used to poison water everywhere in order to deny drinking sources for the guerrillas. Most water pools, rivers and wells which were far away from the villagers would be poisoned. Many people died when they first drank the water without realizing that it was poisoned. Poisoned food was left scattered and one would think it was abandoned. In the Shamva District, many baboons once died because they had eaten poisoned food which was left behind by the soldiers for the guerrillas to take. The freedom fighters knew it was poisoned food. The Rhodesian soldiers also poisoned clothes as they were aware people were giving clothes to the guerrilla forces. Quite a number of freedom fighters who put on such clothes died.

THE CHURCH, EDUCATION AND DEVELOPMENT BEFORE AND AFTER INDEPENDENCE

Before Zimbabwe attained independence in 1980, the role of the Church, in principle, was to evangelize the word of God in practice. Both Catholic and Protestant Churches subscribed to that divine doctrine. The Church in Rhodesia was the first to open, schools, hospitals and introduce better methods of farming among the indigenous people.

The educational system was bottlenecked or pyramid shaped. In primary schools, many African children were enrolled but very few made it to secondary level because the white settlers did not believe Africans were intelligent enough to pass through to secondary school. By 1962, the country had 2 615 primary schools. The primary school education was not a continuum but were two tiered, with five stages at lower primary (Sub A, B, and then Standards 1-3) and Upper Primary (Standards 4-6). Vast numbers of children in the rural areas dropped out of school before they could even complete Standard 3, not because of their financial or intellectual shortcomings, but because the schools were too few.

At secondary school level, there were 22 855 pupils in Standard 6 in 1962, but only 1 987 could find places for Form One; 489 were in Form Two and just 56 could get places for Form Five and Six. Clearly, the colonial regime totally ignored and neglected African education and in some cases openly blocked its expansion. On the contrary, primary education was free for white children and it was a statutory requirement that a white child should receive at least three years of secondary education.

The University of Rhodesia was the only institution of higher learning and opened its doors in 1955. White Rhodesians did not realize that Africans were also intellectually equipped just like any other human being on earth. That is why as early as the 1940s, many Africans from Southern Rhodesia had to continue their university education in the Union of South Africa. On coming back home, the educated blacks were frustrated because they were not offered jobs commensurate with their academic or professional qualifications. The only way to redress was through liberating themselves through the armed struggle. The will was already there to liberate themselves after such physical and psychological violence.

On education, both Protestant and Catholic Missionaries believed in the strategy of opening schools, hospitals and clinics in rural areas. The Dutch Reformed Church, Anglicans, Methodist and Catholic Missionaries started schools around the country, principally, for the local people. Some of these schools include Morgenster, Emapandeni and Chishawasha, St. Augustine, Old Mutare, to mention just a few.

The first mission church at Chishawasha near Harare was opened in 1902. When the Church was officially opened, the young brother of Cecil John Rhodes decided to pay a visit at the Mission. He was both amazed and impressed to see the development which had taken place at the Mission since the arrival of the missionaries in 1890. He remarked how the missionaries had managed to convince, the local people into accepting and participating in developing the school that flourished in gardening, crop farming, orchards and brick moulding. For many years, Chishawasha Mission supplied bricks to the City of Salisbury, all moulded under the instructions and supervision of the Jesuit Brothers and Priests.

One of the famous remarks made by Cecil Rhodes' young brother when he wrote back to England, was that he could not believe what he had seen after travelling through dense bush for

17 miles from Salisbury. He saw this magnificent Church built with well burnt bricks, the green gardens all over as well as green fields and vineyards. Well bred cattle, sheep and goats were something he also marvelled at. All these projects were being done by the Missionaries, teaching and supervising the local people who carried out the work.

After the missionaries had settled at Chishawasha in 1880, a school for boys was opened in1883. The local people were in the habit of protecting their children, but they allowed the boy child to experiment and come to face the new art of reading and writing. The boys were introduced into a new world of artisanship. Some parents became convinced that even the girl child should also benefit from this new life at the mission. So in 1898 under the supervision of the Dominican nuns, the girl child started attending school as well.

Some of the first girls who participated in the experience of the school were the orphaned children whose parents had been killed during the First Chimurenga War. One of these girls was the daughter of Mbuya Nehanda, the famous spirit medium who put up a fierce resistance against the white settlers. She was executed in 1897 together with another spirit medium Sekuru Kaguvi, who was another legendary hero of the First Chimurenga. The tree on which Mbuya Nehanda was hanged is next to the corner of Josiah Tongogara Street and Sam Nujoma (Second Street). It is a sad reminder of the violence perpetrated by the early settlers.

In terms of development, the first plough was introduced by missionaries to the local people. Chishawasha Mission was one of the places where the local people were encouraged to use a plough pulled by spanned oxen. Animal husbandry was also introduced especially after the 1895/6 crisis brought about by rinderpest which was partly the cause of the First Chimurenga.

Missionary Option for Education and Development

After the so called Matabele and Shona rebellion (1893-97), the Missionaries were at loss "as to whether they were doing the right thing or not". It is reported that occasionally, Father Richards visited Chief Chiromba to engage him on the issue of going to war against the settlers. Father Richards proffered advice to the Chief encouraging the Chief and his subjects not to join the war but instead to accept the new dispensation because Africans would eventually be defeated. The Chief assured the Priest that the Africans would join the war but would not attack Chishawasha Mission. It appears that was the reason why the Missionaries declined to go to the Salisbury laager for their own safety and preferred to stay at the Mission throughout the War. Chief Chiromba kept his word and the Missionaries were never attacked by the local people up to the end of the war.

From the bits and pieces of information that has been gathered on the conversations between Chief Chishawasha and Fr Richards, the locals were told not to attack the missionaries but to fight against the settlers who had vowed to conquer and rule over the black people. According to Antony Verrier whose thoughts are captured in his book entitled "*The Road to Zimbabwe (1890-1980)*", the Privy Council declared that Rhodesia was a colony by conquest. So it was very clear in the minds of local people that the settlers had come to settle by force. Violence was inevitable and war was the only option left. One wonders whether the Missionaries did not realise the original objective of the white settlers was to deliberately provoke the local people in order to fight them and conquer them so that the whites could have a legitimate excuse to plunder and loot in the name of recovering what had been lost due to the "rebel-lion".

As mentioned earlier, after the First Chimurenga, the missionaries especially those stationed at Chishawasha had grown wiser. They decided that the best thing for them to do was to carry on with the opening up of more schools and hospitals all over the country for the local people. For the next thirty years, the Catholic Missionaries decided to concentrate and spend more time with the youth at schools and training institutes with the hope that the new generation of local people would eventually appreciate and get used to the new way of life. In that way, Christianity would eventually take root among Africans countrywide. Certainly, that vision and planning was very successful. Until 1947, when the first African school, Goromonzi was opened by the government, several African schools had already been established by missionaries, both Catholic and Protestant.

Education with Production

In general, most mission schools included practical subjects in their syllabus. Some schools put more emphasis on practical subjects than others. For the sake of clarity, most of the training and work mentioned in this book refers mostly to Catholic institutions.

The Catholic Church, spearheaded by the Jesuit Order went on to open the doors of Christianity in what is now Zimbabwe, at the request of the Pope who called it Zambezi Mission early in the 1870s. That religious order of Priest and Brothers (Society of Jesus), popularly known as Jesuits, were the ideal group because they had 400 years of experience in opening new frontiers for the Church all over the world. They had also earned a reputation of "hands- on people" everywhere they went in line with their motto called *"Men for Others"*. They were accompanied by the *Dominican Sisters* who came from South Africa to Rhodesia in June of 1890 along with the Pioneer Column sent by Cecil John Rhodes. Father Prestige was the official Chaplain of the Pioneer Column. This was very surprising indeed in view of the historical Reformation rivalries that an English colonial occupation force (largely Anglican) could accept a Catholic Chaplain instead of an Anglican clergyman!

Apart from Empandeni in Matabeleland (1888), the Catholics also opened two schools in Bulawayo, St. Georges College and Dominican Convent Girls School (1896) for white children in Salisbury. In 1898 the Dominican sisters also opened Chishawasha School (now St Dominic's) for the African girls.

In the education sector, like everywhere else, segregation was rampant. On one hand, there was the African Department and on the other there was the European education system. The same applied to hospitals. There were hospitals for white people only and separate hospitals for Africans. This was institutionalized segregation, violation and violence. Treating people according to the colour of their skin was a macabre act of violence. It left many people with wounded dignity and bruised egos, especially among the black population of that time. It was one of the reasons that spurred young black people to join the Second Chimurenga.

Deliberately, African schools were few and far between especially secondary schools. The colonial regime believed in the myth that Africans did not have the intellectual capacity to pass. Before the advent of independence (in 1980) some Africans studied through (private studying) in order to complete secondary education.

After a devastating war which destroyed many educational institutions, a multifaceted approach to the education system was needed, this was dubbed Education with Development. Sadly, it was not the case in the new Zimbabwe. It was a back to life-as-usual. Besides the reconstruction of destroyed old roads, bridges and buildings, old human habits and attitudes prevailed in the new order. This is sometimes referred to as "colonial hang-over".

The educational system in the country was characterized by racial segregation which colonial Rhodesia institutionalized. The new Zimbabwe came up with a new philosophy in education. The Ministry of Education coined the motto *"education with production"*. It was accepted in principle, but implementation has been slow. To a large extend, the institutions still produce a mass of job seekers who naturally become very hungry but educated young people. As a result, they become breeding ground for perpetrators of new waves of violence because of lack of employment as what happened in the colonial past.

On the eve of Independence (17 April 1980), the new Prime Minister, Robert Gabriel Mugabe, made an outstanding speech when he proclaimed the policy of national reconciliation. That speech stunned nearly everyone and the rest of the world was dumbfounded. The media which had always labelled him as a tyrant and terrorist were also shocked. Most of his critics were calling him a "Saint". The pronouncement of the reconciliation policy was a great achievement to the nation in varying degrees and from different perspectives. It disarmed those citizens who were sharpening their swords for vengeance and it also created confidence and a sense of security to those who were caught unawares on the unfolding dramatic events of 18 April 1980.

On the day when polling results were announced some of white members of the community were frightened to go back home from work because they feared their domestic workers would probably assault them now that there was a new black government in power. The author took it upon himself to advise the police to issue a public statement through the media assuring all citizens that all was well. The Minister called on the police to move around offices telling people (many whites) to go home and enjoy the dawn of a new era because nobody would be harmed.

Sadly, the proclamation of the reconciliation policy was treated as an event not as a process which should have been followed through. The full cycle for reconciliation should have been: **Reconciliation, Rehabilitation** and **Reconstruction.**

Reconciliation, Rehabilitation, Reconstruction

Reconciliation – Most white Rhodesians were a community of die-hard racists. The crude and spineless ones left the country quickly - but not without leaving a trail of destruction. Some black Zimbabweans whose dignity and self esteem had long been shattered by colonial subjugation continued to regard themselves as inferior to their whites counterparts. Such attitudes led to dire political consequences later as time went on.

Zimbabwe's past can only be understood through the prism of the present. It follows that strategies adopted at independence and the post independence dissident era, will inevitably shape current political and social contexts. The past can not be ignored because past traumas have emotional results for an individual and society at a later stage. It follows that process of strategic planning in terms of identification of either ethnic or racial communities across the political divide; social and cultural groups should have been made. The electronic and print media should have highlighted attitudinal changes to enable people to forgive each other and live in harmony.

National events, where people would meet and socialize could have also helped the long process of nation building. Introduction of civic programmes and workshops specifically to foster national reconciliation would have had positive results in healing the wounds. Clarity of purposes as to why it was necessary to carry out programmes on reconciliation and peaceful co-existence between ethnic groups could have had a positive impact on Zimbabwean society.

Montville who carried out a study of political violence argues that those who have suffered unjustified violence have an enduring fear of the trauma recurring, a fear which undermines the possibility of developing renewed trust in their tormentors. This inhibits any true healing or eventual reintegration. Montville went further to emphasize that the passage of time (silence over extended period) does not heal all the wounds or any wound at all. Instead, wounds associated with acknowledged and unforgiven past are often passed to the following generations thereby creating a gap of fear, entrenchment and hatred.

As it turned out, it became a one sided affair, a good political strategy which failed to win the hearts and minds of all Zimbabweans. Inferiority and superiority complexes have remained entrenched among and between citizens up to the present time. In fact, had there been spiritual and social reconciliation, then, the land question would have been resolved amicably and equitably. Reconciliation without rehabilitation became a lonely affair.

Rehabilitation – According to Webster's Dictionary, rehabilitation means to restore to a former capacity, to restore to a state of efficiency and good management.

In the case of the people of Zimbabwe who were involved in a guerrilla war which went on for fifteen years, the need for rehabilitation and psychologically guiding people away from a war situation cannot be over-emphasized. People used to be alert all the time because danger and death lurked in the shadows. For them to accept normalcy so suddenly becomes a vexing matter. Such a situation certainly needed rehabilitation from war to peace, without any suspicions.

The integration of ex-combatants into civilian life was never done. Some ex-fighters came back from war to find that their families had been wiped out and homes destroyed while others were welcomed by half the family still alive, the other half had perished in the same war in which they had fought. For a warrior returning home, it was a psychological crisis and nightmare to accept the new realities brought by the end of the war because they were used to very mobile life styles and accustomed to unpredictable circumstances.

For those soldiers who served in the RSF, they were used to a life of propaganda and psychological warfare. Segregation between white and black soldiers in the armed forces had been accepted by black soldiers and so was the standard of life. So the complexes of superiority and inferiority remained. The real issues at stake were that when a situation arose which was prompted by misunderstandings, violent reaction ensued. Some family disputes ended tragically, as family members resorted to violence, which often led to loss of life. Even those people who were too young to remember the war, simply because they were growing up in a potentially violent environment, and brought up by people who participated in the armed conflict, such children may end up in the vicious circle of violence. It has been established by psychologists that even a baby learns certain behavioural traits while it is still in their mother's womb. It follows that, victims of violence often end up as the perpetrators of violence. In Zimbabwe the nation faces the reality of the consequences of an orgy of violence as a result of the war.

In the post independence period, Churches and social groups did not take racial segregation as a serious issue that needed to be rectified. Churches were aware of the existence of racial prejudice but they never bothered to address the rehabilitation issue, in order to start a new era. The white population started moving away from the neighbourhood where the black middle class had moved in. Rehabilitation was not only necessary but imperative among the whites for them to be able to accept the changing circumstance.

The attitude of the former Rhodesian whites towards blacks shaped the attitude of some of the white commercial farmers when the land question came to the fore in 2000. The whole idea of having to share the land with blacks was unacceptable even if it was a fact that the whites in colonial Rhodesia had acquired such land through violence. Other white farmers had the financial wherewithal offered by racial preference that enabled them to borrow from banks and financial institutions to fund their agricultural activities.

Racial privilege which the whites enjoyed from the beginning of the nation state of Rhodesia (1890 – 1980) had became part of their culture. Those privileges became **Rights** - special rights, endowed upon them by virtue of being white. It never crossed their minds that they were a privileged small community enjoying benefits at the expense of the blacks who were the majority.

If there had been a serious social rehabilitation programmes for the whites together with their black counter parts, then tensions and apprehension could have died down. By so doing, the demands by government for land from whites, in order to share it with the landless blacks, would have been resolved amicably. In fact, the willing buyer - willing seller approach could have been acceptable and championed by both the State and white commercial farmers. Such positive collaboration between Government and white commercial farmers with the backing of the international community could have assisted Zimbabwe.

Lack of social rehabilitation kept the Rhodesians in their laager of ignorance. They could not read the danger warning signs of an impending volatile and explosive situation over land. Any political sensitive person could have realized that from 1981, the local people who were genuinely landless used to invade white commercial farms every year. The violent method of acquiring land was largely because of the failure to study history from the underside where the majority belonged. The upper side of the history in Zimbabwe has become defective and incomplete.

Reconstruction - War destroys everything in its wake from humans to infrastructure. The philosophy of reconstruction in Zimbabwe lacked a creative adjustment to contemporary (new) conditions by cultivating a tradition with a new face in a new era. Failure to learn or discover the causes of armed conflict for 15 years by the Rhodesians, blinded many of them, especially those who owned land. The truth of the matter is that the armed conflict in Zimbabwe was principally over land and self determination. When the war ended, the reconstruction of the economy and physical infrastructure followed the old Rhodesian ways and habits. Even the blacks who had fought the war of liberation just moved into the former Protected Villages because their family homes had been destroyed.

In the mid 1980s, responding to the failure of the resettlement exercise, landless peasants began to occupy and use land that belonged to the politicians and black elite. These new occupants were termed "squatters" by the media, and in some areas army and police units were deployed to violently and forcibly remove them. Bulldozers and trucks were used to raze their dwellings to the ground and many peasants were arrested Reminiscent of the forced eviction and destruction of property by the colonial state 40 years earlier, the 'squatters' were crushed ruthlessly.

The Matabeleland region and parts of the Midlands witnessed an exceptional degree of this violence as crops were burnt, and villagers were brutally murdered soon after independence. Some disgruntled former ZIPRA combatants absconded from the newly integrated Zimbabwe National Army and began to terrorize people in the villages in what became known as the "dissident campaign. In response, the Government deployed the Korean trained Fifth Brigade to deal with the situation.

Atrocities perpetrated by the Fifth Brigade in its attempt to crush the "dissidents" were subsumed by a wider and brutal struggle against insurgency of ex-ZIPRA combatants. The inhabitants of Matabeleland were regarded as part of the problem by the government and by the time when ink was put to paper to seal the Unity Accord between ZAPU and Zanu-PF in1987, an estimated 6 000 *(the figure 20 000 is peddled on the Internet see Breaking the Silence document)* people had been either killed or injured (This is a conservative figure as it is believed that a larger number lost their lives or were injured). The dissident campaign was in many ways a continuation of the ideological and ethnic conflict between the liberation armies of ZIPRA and ZANLA transposed to post independence Zimbabwe. The genesis of the violence can be traced back to the 19th Century ethnic struggles between the Shona and Amandebele tribes.

The reconstruction failed to overhaul and reorganize the national governance system and re-establishment of government command structures. The thrust of the economy, previously tailormade for the minority white community continued. Economic and political violence in Zimbabwe which continued to the present day today is traced to the failed reconstruction of the

1980s. The reconstruction and transformation process from Rhodesia to Zimbabwe was painstakingly difficult. The structures and systems adopted in the reconstruction period returned the country back to its previous master and servant ideology. The previous "owners" of the economy, the minority whites and a few blacks were gap- fillers. Some cosmetic changes were made in the fields of health, education and removal of jobs reserved for whites only. These were mostly service provisions not economic empow.erment or ownership.

The new realities in the post war period after 1980, should have been taken into account by both those who lost political power but still remained in charge of the economy, on one hand, and those won who had assumed the reigns of the State power, but still without economic power. Such structural challenges needed commitment, cooperation and political will to address the widening gap between the haves and the have-nots and dispensing with the underlying suspicions that breed violence. That approach could have forged an undertaking to redress. the economic anomalies gradually, but sadly, it did not happen.

The faith community should not be absolved from blame because of its dismal failure to inculcate civic education among and between its followers before and after independence. The delivery of civic education could have resulted in social harmony, peace building, tolerance and ultimately national development. Civic education could have changed people's minds because once a nation has adequately grounded civic education; it becomes easier resolve national challenges. Those victims who still harbour hatred in their minds are able to cast hatred aside through civic education.

A happy, progressive and prosperous nation can not be built as long as men and women continue to have ill feelings emanating from their painful past. Admittedly, racial hatred and violence were practiced and remain part and parcel of the history of Zimbabwe. That should now be forgiven and forgotten. People have suffered enough from bitterness and that too should be forgotten for the nation to move forward.

In hindsight, the violent journey that has been travelled from Rhodesia to Zimbabwe was poorly managed and consequently, hatched a monster in the form of an aggressive and violent generation. To redress that violent behaviour at national level, government ought to supervise and invest in peacemaking. Otherwise without that, the spiral of violence will recur unabated.

MATABELELAND AND MIDLANDS DISTURBANCES

The ten years before and after independence in Zimbabwe, negatively affected the Matabeleland and Midlands provinces. The decade prior to independence witnessed an increasingly violent war of liberation, whilst the post independence decade caused further hardships and suffering in Matabeleland and in parts of the Midlands. The people in those provinces, who had survived the protracted war of liberation, soon faced yet another orgy of violence, this time being perpetrated by their own government. It was a matter of being thrown out of the pan into the furnace.

The Legacy of ZANU – ZAPU Antagonism

In 1963, a political rift between Joshua Nkomo, then president of the Zimbabwe African People's Union (ZAPU) and mostly Shona speaking leaders emerged. This led to the split in ZAPU and formation of ZANU (Zimbabwe African National Union) led by Reverend Ndabaningi Sithole. A complex inter-play of factors led to this rift. Those factors involved not only policy but personal differences between the nationalist leaders. This was coupled with a policy of "divide and rule" instigated by the white Rhodesian regime, which put a wedge within the nationalist movement formations. Aspects of the early split had negative implications for peace during and after the liberation war. The "burden of history" of that antagonism had far reaching implications for post colonial political developments especially in the military crackdown perpetrated by the Shona speaking Fifth Brigade in Matabeleland in the early 1980s. It is historically argued that ZANU –ZAPU political rivalry which bred violence in modern day Zimbabwe was a continuation of the 19th century invasions of Mashonaland by the Amandebele.

The 1963 split was followed by fierce fighting between ZANLA and ZIPRA in training camps in Tanzania and on the front, in Zimbabwe. These clashes frequently resulted in many casualties and left a marked legacy of distrust between the two liberation armies and their political wings. Subsequently, the liberation war began to assume a noticeably distinct ethnic composition. None of the two movements was ethnically homogeneous. However, ZANU and ZANLA were mostly Shona, whilst ZAPU and ZIPRA were predominantly Ndebele. The movements used ethnicity as a political and military tool to gain support of the masses and thus intensified ethnicity. Distinct "self-identification" among the peasants and guerrillas not only emerged, but intensified.

Although these two forces succeeded in sending the message home that Zimbabweans needed freedom, the politicization of ethnicity had potential negative implications for lasting peace in post independence Zimbabwe. The protracted conflict which had begun during the fight for liberation would resurface again during the integration of the RSF, ZANLA and ZIPRA forces soon after independence.

The formation of the Zimbabwe National Army (ZNA) was not smooth. The biggest challenge facing the newly elected government related to the integration of erstwhile enemies (ZANLA, ZIPRA and the RSF) into one national defence force. This was particularly the case since the liberation fighters felt they had all it took to form the defence force by themselves. However, the bulk of the officer corps and the rank and file soldiers ended up being extracted from ZANLA forces. The retention of the RSF had a significant cost with regards to the formation of the ZNA and nation-building. As noted earlier, the RSF had conducted brutal counter-insurgence operations which included the indiscriminate killing of civilians and the use of torture. The RSF personnel were then pardoned through a blanket amnesty by the new government on the basis that their crimes had been committed in a time of war and thus should be "bygones" The major problems of the post colonial state were that it was incapable of mediating between competing and contenting forces within its society. Sadly, the message sent by the leadership was that the security forces would benefit from the same impunity enjoyed by their Rhodesian predecessors.

Apparently, the retention of the RSF personnel in the new security sector had its parallel in the legal sphere. The newly elected government inherited and preserved the State of Emergency and the Law and Order Maintenance Act in their entirety. During the State of Emergency, the State had the exclusive powers to imprison anyone without trial. The failure by the new government to find an acceptable power-sharing formula and to resolve questions like pan-ethnic solidarity and building a truly national army, reflective of ethnic considerations, led to the post colonial state to be intransigent and to use the repressive machinery inherited from Rhodesia.

However, and to the contrary, clashes erupted between ex-ZANLA and ex-ZIPRA forces, mostly in Assembly Points dotted around the country where the freedom fighters temporarily stayed awaiting either demobilization or integration into the ZNA. According to available accounts, the fighting was instigated by an inflammatory speech made in Bulawayo by Enos Nkala, a ZANU PF Minister. In the speech Nkala categorically threatened that he would crush the ZAPU leader Dr Joshua Nkomo.

The recurrence of violence in assembly points saw Prime Minister Robert Mugabe announcing that there were sinister undertones organized by ZAPU and ZIPRA. As a result, victimization of some ZIPRA and ZAPU elements was witnessed in the military and political structures. That victimization led to the exodus of ZIPRA forces from the ZNA ranks. The desertions also led to the perceived notion by ZANU leaders that ZAPU wanted to overthrow the government.

Emergence of Dissidents

The much craved for, and anticipated peace and tranquillity, did not come as the newly independent state experienced and suffered a new wave of violence in the Midlands and Matabeleland regions.

The spectre of political violence after independence   by political groups which lost in the elections was based upon the premise that, since Zanu-PF was ruling, it had successful waged a formidable armed struggle, where it was equally essential for who wanted to snatch power, and eventually rule, to use the same means to dislodge ZANU PF from power. Consequently, during the defining moment of the newly independent state, the government failed to monopolize its control over the means of violence. What then followed was an orgy of violence and violation.

The defection of some of the former ZIPRA cadres from the ZNA started after some misunderstanding with the ruling party and Government. Dissident operations in Matabeleland and the Midlands is a living story which needs to be clarified for the future generations not to repeat similar mistakes.

Many issues remained clouded and classified. There is nothing mysterious about the Matabeleland disturbances; As already mentioned, people know what happened but they do not want to explain why it happened because of fear. Many people who were behind the original cause as to WHY it happened are still alive. Just as some of the people who participated in the attempt to crush dissident operation militarily, and some former dissents themselves are still alive. They can tell their story as individuals. But in order to close the chapter, it is necessary that some of those who know or were responsible for master minding the original plan should honour this country by giving an honest account of what happened. Such an honour would put the two communities of Shona and Amandebele to rest and destroy any ethnical hatred and suspicions which continues to simmer. Such political violence between PFZapu and Zanu-PF from 1989- 1987 left wounded souls and humiliated human dignity which is too gruesome to forget. This is one of the negative legacies of the liberation war. Rhodesians easily compare the two tragedies and shamefully blame the later on the "blacks". Such type of dismissive approach and attitude towards a wounded people would never assist to heal the nation, emotionally, socially and spiritually.

Deployment of the Fifth Brigade

The Fifth Brigade was deployed in 1983 in Matabeleland. This deployment saw unprecedented forms of terror and hardships being perpetrated on the civilian population. The Brigade's actions were short but sharp. Its exercise of violence was concentrated within a short time and within a limited geographical area. The Brigade justified its operation and violence against the civilians in Matabeleland in explicitly tribal and political terms. It not only systematically attacked ZAPU and other community leaders but it also attacked civilians, the police, civil servants, and even members of the ZNA. In some instances it evoked pre-colonial memories of Ndebele raids on the Shona and regarded itself as a Shona defence force which had come to revenge on the Ndebele's historical transgressions against their Shona ancestry. As such, nothing was spared. It targeted every Ndebele man, woman and child and was especially aggressive to ZAPU and its related structures.

The Fifth Brigade operations in Matabeleland saw the reestablishment of bases at schools, boreholes, police stations, clinics and in mountains. In those bases, various atrocities were committed by members of the Brigade. Villagers were detained, tortured and murdered. The Fifth Brigade also made forays away from the bases. There were no wards in which atrocities were not committed. Some however, suffered more than others. The villages of Lupane Valley had the largest number of people killed. The thickly forested areas along the Shangani River were also targeted mainly because they were havens for dissidents, displaced villagers and large numbers of ZAPU youths. The most notorious detention base was Bhalangwe in Kezi. The locals called this base a "concentration camp". According to various sources, four to five people were reportedly beaten to death by the Fifth Brigade soldiers. The killers openly admitted that their business was to kill.

The Fifth Brigade also resorted to aggressive and yet abhorrent "political mobilization and re-orientation "campaigns". In an attempt to win the hearts and minds of the villagers, locals were forced to attend political meetings in the ZANLA way of "*pungwes*" (night meetings). At these meetings, the people of the affected areas were forced to chant Zanu-PF slogans, produce Zanu-PF party membership cards, sing Zanu-PF related songs and denounce ZAPU. The 5th Brigade actions were motivated by both ethnic and political considerations. The Brigade wanted to wipe out the entire Ndebele ethnic tribe and in the process destroying ZAPU's political base.

The Brigade also used food as both a military and political weapon. Its operations included depriving villagers of food through the closure of grinding mills, stores and burning granaries. The aim was to destroy the villagers' will to exist as a political entity.

The consequences of these draconian actions were that ethnic prejudice was hardened. A strong link between ethnicity and political affiliation was also enforced. The military and political crackdown alienated the AmaNdebele people from the State and ensured extremely negative civil military relations. The legacy of the violence committed by the Brigade continues to shape politics in Zimbabwe today.

The way in which the violence was unleashed was unexpected, sudden, profound and unprecedented. Having experienced such horrific atrocities, civilians in the affected areas still believe it could happen again.

Results of Organized Violence in Matabeleland

The repressive violence did not only affect individuals but terrorized the whole community. The destruction of traditional social, political and economic structures by both the colonial and post independence state run through the history of the Ndebele like a thread. These measures often led to mass deaths and suffering.

The affected people still suffer from psychological, economic and physical wounds inflicted upon them by their own government. These wounds have not healed despite efforts by government not to open up these wounds. These wounds if not attended to are a time-bomb.

The people of Matabeleland still feel that true national reconciliation, healing and integration do not exist. They are still worried about the resumption of state-sponsored violence even with the formation of the inclusive government.

POLITICAL PARTIES, ECONOMIC INSECURITIES AND VIOLENCE

The political landscape in Zimbabwe since 1980 has been unique compared to other countries on the African continent. Besides South Africa, Zimbabwe was the only country which had such a large number of white legislators (20 seats). It was a Parliament which was quite lively in the early 1980's. The majority of the legislators were made up of former freedom fighters facing their former white enemies, retired territorial soldiers and a few former African politicians who had joined the so-called "Internal Settlement" namely Bishop Abel Muzorewa, Reverend Ndabaningi Sithole and Chief Jeremiah Chirau.

The politics of Zimbabwe unlike other former British colonies and protectorates had deep-seated attitude of conquest by the former colonial masters. Those masters influenced the white community apportioning to them, a sense of self esteem because the economy, infrastructure, commerce and industry; the financial services sector; as well as professional and technical manpower base, were still in their hands.

The 20 white entrenched seats in Parliament accorded to the whites by the Lancaster House Agreement, served a purpose, for long ten years in which they could not be tempered with. All the 20 white Members of Parliament were seasoned legislators. Even though they were few in number, their familiarity with legislative procedures and the international contacts they had established over the years, made them an very effective and powerful minority.

The Rhodesia Front (RF) was re-christened the "Republican Front Party", and then renamed again as the "Conservative Alliance" (CA) until it vanished into thin air. Apart from the new party names, they carried on with the philosophy of kaffir-master attitude. Some of the whites were still celebrating 11 November which was the anniversary of the 1965 Unilateral Declaration of Independence (UDI). That was the fulfilment of the doctrine that "*Rhodesians Never Die*". The RF was an all white political outfit in a predominantly black country. Political objectives of the white RF were at variance with the aspirations of the new political dispensation led by Zanu-PF unless there was lasting racial integration. In essence, there was never any racial integration or any attempt nor plan to implement it even though there was the official reconciliation proclamation by the Prime Minister. The response to the hand of reconciliation was "*you may take any African from the bush but you cannot take the bush out of the African*". Such racial attitudes could not, and will never bring about peaceful co-existence across the racial divide.

Gradually, the RF died a natural death before it had managed to help the small, but economically strong white community, to integrate into the new social order of an independent and sovereign Zimbabwe. Had this happened, Zimbabwe could have become a shining example of racial integration in the world.

Post Unity Accord Politics: 1987 – 2000

Anyone who has followed the political events in Zimbabwe since 1957, and thereafter, would agree that the differences between ZAPU and ZANU, as revolutionary political parties, were very artificial. The rivalries were, to a large extend based principally on political approach and personalities. The philosophy of the two parties, in terms of ideology and political objectives were the basically the same. Those who had the privilege of working with the two political organizations and their armed wings during the struggle can testify the truth in this assertion. Apart from occasional and rare tension between the two groups, even the Organization of African Unity (OAU) and the United Nations were basically happy with their operations and relationship. The Patriotic Front (PF) became a reality because most of the leadership from either party, ZAPU or ZANU were old friends and comrades in arms. The Unity Accord of 1987, which brought political tranquillity in the country, was agreed upon without much acrimony. Later that political tranquillity became political sterility among some political cadres.

Unity brought peace, but it also brought laziness, lethargy and corruption because of the absence of a strong political opposition. Many citizens were frustrated. Even complaints made to the highest authorities, about misuse of public funds, abuse of political positions, incompetence were ignored. Productivity plummeted as corruption by some of those in authority was not nipped in the bud. Many senior public servants and veteran politicians including some Cabinet Ministers were routinely "recycled" and remained in the system. Even some of those who should have, under normal circumstances, offered to resign because of their poor performance or corrupt activities, still hung on to their jobs as if nothing had happened. Even the courtesy to apologize to the public for wrongdoing as is normally practiced in other countries, was never done. Impunity became the order of the day.

The patience of the people was running out and citizens were seeking political alternatives. It will not be forgotten that Zanu-PF as a political party, had, for decades, made many sacrifices. The party gave birth to the new nation through an armed struggle. But the tendency by some of the leaders was to take people for granted could not be tolerated *ad infinitum*. For the leaders to use their liberation war credentials as passports to looting national assets is also wrong.

From this stand point, apart from mounting external influence and pressure brought to bear on the authorities as a result of the land reform, Zanu-PF invited a protest vote from some of the citizens during the 2000 referendum which gave birth to the opposition Movement for Democratic Change that garnered support from the electorate largely in urban centres. It was a rude awakening for many in the ruling party, who were shocked by results of the plebiscite, particularly those who were complacent and ignored the reality on the ground that they had lost to the opposition.

Intolerance

The reality of having a strong opposition political party after the Unity Accord should have not been a surprise to Zanu-PF, taking into account the very fact that Zimbabwe was already a multiparty state. Opposition political parties, which included the United African National Congress (UANC), Zimbabwe Unity Movement (ZUM), SUPER ZAPU, to mention but a few, had been in existence. At some point it was preferred to have a strong but patriotic opposition party. An opposition party is vital because it keeps checks and balances in the ruling party in all constituencies. Legislators in their constituencies would be compelled to fulfil the promises which they made when they canvassed for elections, otherwise they would lose the next election. What then went wrong with the emergence of the youthful Movement for Democratic Change (MDC)?

The swiftness with which the new party candidates contested seats over night and unseated some of the long standing, overconfident, political stalwarts, shocked even the MDC contestants themselves. However, the truth was that the new party could not sustain itself without the financial support from white farmers and industrialists. Quick reaction to an unfamiliar political environment caused some of the violation and violence which followed especially in the year 2000. Some of the members within the opposition MDC party were prepared to retaliate when attacked. Another wave of violence had come back to haunt Zimbabwe. In many instances it was difficult to establish who was fanning the violence or who had provoked the other.

Sometimes dirty tricks took place in the form of some youths dressed in their political opponents' regalia. They would attack and destroy properties of their political rivals. Practical examples were those of state run buses ferrying children who were using arms of war in typical modern military style. New buses were also attacked and set on fire. In retaliation the police and other state functionaries in charge of security reacted swiftly, arresting and detaining suspects. Others were killed in the ensuing violence. An example was Cain Nkala (ZANU PF) and MDC polling agent Talent Mabika together with Tichaona Chimenya, the official driver of MDC President, Morgan Tsvangirai were killed when their vehicle was petrolbombed in Buhera District by a known assailant in April 2000.

Politically motivated violence during the run up to Parliamentary and Presidential elections was also witnessed. The 2000 referendum followed by Parliamentary elections was confused with the land occupations which were taking place at the same time. The land occupations and the political violence even confused the violators themselves. From reports by some youths who had been apprehended by police, it was clear that the youths were sponsored by political candidates or militant party supporters.

The presidential campaign of 2002 was equally clouded by politically motivated violence. The political leadership of both Zanu-PF and MDC parties admitted that fact. The police had detailed and well-documented evidence of such violent activities and the parties they belong, and the type of violence each perpetrator had committed.

Usually pre-election violence is committed by possible losers, whilst post election violence can be started by either the losers who refuse to accept defeat or it can also be started by the winners who want to settle old scores by visiting vengeance against their competitors. The implications of such violence are that it dehumanises and engenders feelings of hatred among and between the people. The unresolved anger begets more violence and the cycle continues.

Increased Militancy

After the 1978 Internal Agreement by the African leadership of Muzorewa, Sithole and Chirau, three auxiliary armies were set up. Muzorewa had 9 000, Sithole with 6 000 and Chirau with 3 000 forces. These were called bully boys. On top of it, ZANLA, ZIPRA and the RSF was also operating in the country. By mid-1978, they were six different armies operating in Zimbabwe. Most of them were still very young and the impact of military training had a negative bearing on them in the future.

Later, those 'young militants' were demobilised to join civilian society without adequate rehabilitation. Their state of mind had not been demobilized at the onset, and such people could easily re-mobilize into the so-called militia bases because of their past experiences which still haunted them. Auxiliary forces of the UANC were all males. Some of them preyed on young girls whom they gangraped. This shows what young people with a military background and unstable mind can do. The situation was reminiscent of the 1960s when youths drank beer and smoked marijuana (mbanje) and under influence they would engage in internicine violence. That violent period was called *'ndoita madiro'* (I do as I please!). Violent acts such as rape, beatings and damage to property were committed by marauding youths particularly in African townships. Since Rhodesia was a police state, the trigger-happy policeman would then shoot the youth gangs with impunity.

Lack of political maturity, indiscipline and ignorance led to increased agitation and militancy especially among the youths in the run up to 2000 elections. The right to mobilise and canvass for political support by the youths of different parties was not "allowed". Some places, especially in rural areas became "no go areas" for the opposition. In such areas, except for the ruling Zanu-PF, other political parties were unable to propagate their views or canvass for support without fear of intimidation and harassment. Respect, tolerance, dignity and decency were thrown out of the window.

The consequence of such violent behaviour was evaporation of investor confidence after violent demonstrations. Political recruitment of young cadres by parties missed out on how to find honest, self respecting young people whose moral aptitude forbad them from engaging in hooliganism. Those violent young people who were recruited were supplied with drugs and beer flowed incessantly for them to have Dutch courage to commit crimes without any sense of shame. This turned young people into beasts and zombies.

Recruitment for the liberation struggle did not select good from bad young recruits, but there was strict discipline in the training camps. However, the true colours of the cadres were later discovered. The price of mass recruitment from guerrilla training was sometimes very high. These were lessons that were not learnt by the entire nation and that is why Zimbabwe continues to suffer.

From interviews conducted and oral comments made by ordinary people in the streets, regardless of the political divide, senior politicians sent their children for further education overseas or in neighbouring countries, but the same politicians mobilized the neighbour's children who, were in the country and recruit them for political assignments of a violent nature. Such consciousness by the majority of citizens will only be recognized when they are given a political platform where they can share such experiences and expose such abuse.

People were not so sure about the political ramifications of joining a particular political party. So to be on the "safe" side, many people ended up with different political party membership cards. One hoped that any approaching groups of campaigners would be identifiable while the person would be able to pull out the correct membership card and claim to the group to be one of them! This was done to ensure safety from some rough, rude and violent political activists. Others got the opportunity of getting financial and material gain by belonging to many political parties. Where some political parties were distributing goods such as bicycles, clothes, food, and money, to their card carrying supporters, the multiparty cardholder benefited immensely from all political parties. If violence broke out, in situations where the "deal" had not been discovered, the practice gave those who benefited more courage to continue to do so in future.

OPERATION MURAMBATSVINA

The Government-sponsored scotched earth policy or blitz codenamed Operation Murambatsvina (*Drive out trash*) and military intervention in Matabeleland and parts of midlands soon after independence affirmed the repressive nature of the ruling political elite. All kinds of theories have been advanced to explain the response by the State to national security, one thing was clear; the crackdown was evocative of the government's well-documented history of reckless abuse of power and repressive tendencies.

Whatever the real motives for the two operations were, ZANU PF only succeeded in reinforcing its credentials as an authoritarian administration that abuses state power. The party and government had fundamentally shifted from being a revolutionary liberator to being repressive. While the state was duty bound to guarantee national security this did not happen in Zimbabwe. For realization of human security goals, the State had at its disposal many policy options. The absence of an effective state machinery or its lack of effectiveness can be detrimental to human security.

Initially this Chapter outlines the scope and impact of Operation Murambatsvina, a crackdown on illegal residential structures in urban centres. In Shona, Murambatsvina means *Drive out filth*. Then *Gukurahundi*, which means *the Storm that sweeps chaff follows*. It was a sting military operation against dissident elements from former ZIPRA who were responsible for disturbances in Matebeleland.and parts of Midlands.

Background of Operation Murambatsvina

After the 31 March 2005 elections, **ZANU PF** felt threatened because the opposition **MDC** had wrestled from it, many constituencies which had belonged to the ruling party in previous elections. The media reported that intelligence operatives unveiled a plan to nip in the bud a Ukrainian-style orange revolution (or street protests), which the opposition was reportedly organizing.

Perhaps by design, and also the prevailing socio-political dynamics, ZANU PF developed an intolerant form of nationalism dictated by a selective mix of class, ethnic and ideological interests. The party's uncanny brand of nationalism grew increasingly intolerant of the diversity of viewpoints and freedom of expression then viciously attacked any form of dissent or criticism. This then led to divisions of patriot/traitor and citizen/alien relations among and between its supporters and also directed at the opposition.

Many other motivations behind Operation Murambatsvina were raised and included among others:

- Increased chaos and congestion especially in Harare high density suburbs which was fast losing its *"Sunshine City"* status;
- Retribution against people and areas known by Zanu-PF to have voted for the opposition during the previous parliamentary and presidential elections "a pre-emptive strategy; tailored to prevent an uprising in the view of deepening food insecurity and other economic hardships;
- The ill-advised move and brutal crackdown on citizens unleashed far-reaching consequences on the national psyche and body politic.

The Launch of Operation Murambatsvina

The first official launch of Operation Murambatsvina, which started on 19 May 2005 was announced by the Chairperson of the Government appointed Harare Commission, Ms Sekesai Makwavarara. Reminiscent of the RSF operations that razed rural villages to the ground in colonial Rhodesia, the teams embarked on a "crack" operation on cities, towns, growth points and mining areas. Although it started from the capital city Harare, the crackdown rapidly spread across the country demolishing and evicting residents leaving them homeless in the middle of winter. State security agencies which conducted the blitz included the army, police and intelligence officials. Because of its harshness, speed and ferocity, the affected citizens called it "Operation Tsunami".

During the launch, Ms Makwavarara emphasized that the programme was to enforce the Regional Town and Country Planning Act (which had been enacted in 1976 by the colonial regime to keep African out of urban areas) to stop all forms of illegal activities which included among others, vending, trading in foreign exchange and illegal dwellings.

Harare residents were ordered to destroy the illegal structures which they had erected by themselves before June 20, 2005. However, on 25 May, in complete disregard of the official deadline, a huge military-style operation started in Harare spreading to Bulawayo, Chitungwiza, Mutare, Rusape, Masvingo, Murehwa and Kadoma. In theory, the state was responsible for protecting its citizens, yet that episode of state repression was still carried out. Far more people suffered at the hands of their own government. Repression by the state in its various forms became a source of insecurity, intimidation and fear.

Scope and Impact of Murambatsvina

In practice, the primary responsibility of the State is to protect and provide human security to its citizens and, by extension, prevent threats and harm on them. Accordingly, the state should not and must withdraw from this sacred obligation. In 2005, this was not the case in Zimbabwe. Operation Murambatsvina had a negative impact on Zimbabweans economically, socially, institutionally and politically. Not only did this operation result in macabre ripple effects, but also its violent effects that are felt up to the present time and will continue to haunt victims in future.

Many houses, tuck-shops, market stalls, flea-markets, vegetable-markets hair saloons and many residential structures were destroyed in a well orchestrated pattern of repression. Most of these informal structures had sprung up because by the mid 1990s, Zimbabwe began to witness rising unemployment caused by the Economic Structural Adjustment Programme (ESAP). Sensing danger, the government allowed the informal sectors to sprout through a series of policy measures. Those policies saw the reduction of previously regulatory bottlenecks to allow new and mainly indigenous entrepreneurs to start commercial distribution sector and also production of goods and services. In implementing this policy, physical planning requirements were relaxed. As stated earlier, Statutory Instrument 216 of 1994 of the Regional Town and Country Planning Act, which allowed for springing up and development of non-residential activities (especially in the high density suburbs, was relaxed.

The relaxation of Statutory Instrument 216 gave most of the people who had been affected by ESAP an opportunity to fend for their families through small scale commercial and industrial activities. Special consent was also given to small scale industries employing between five to ten people, in welding, shoe repair, carpentry and motor industries. By 2004, a thriving informal sector that accounted for 40% of employment had been established.

During that period, the informal sector had effectively become the mainstay of the majority of the urban population, 70% of whom were estimated to be officially unemployed and 75% of them living below the poverty datum line.

Besides home industries, flea-markets and vending stores, most of the urban areas throughout Zimbabwe had witnessed the growth of street hawkers and make-shift stands. Many of these hawkers sold their goods in front of formal shops, clearly violating the rights of established the formal sector which was paying taxes to the government. There was chaos, confusion, congestion and jostling especially in the Central Business District (CBD) of Harare. This confusion was blamed on the government by the owners of the formal businesses.

Harare soon lost its lustre. In an effort to preserve that sunshine status, running battles between the hawkers and the Harare Municipal Police were witnessed. In some places, the Zimbabwe Republic Police (ZRP) was called in to quell violent clashes. In that mayhem, goods that hawkers were selling were destroyed or confiscated by both ZRP and municipal police. This angered the already impoverished urban poor. Their only means of survival had been destroyed, leaving them without any means of survival to fend for their families.

Demographically, urban centers in Zimbabwe witnessed a rapid population growth of 5 percent per annum throughout the 1980s. This strained the capacities of both the local and central governments to provide basic amenities to the poor. Interdependent conditions such as hunger, poor health services, environmental and political problems then set in. A series of both internal and external events were also experienced further contributing to the vicious circle.

These events included, among others:

- The compensation of war veterans for their services during the liberation struggle. In 1997, the veterans of the liberation struggle were awarded $50 000.00 each as compensation for their services during and after the struggle. The Zimbabwean dollar immediately crashed and inflation set in;
- A bitterly disputed fast-track land reform programme, which had been implemented in the year 2000, saw the exchange of land from white commercial farmers to new inexperienced black farmers. The black farmers were not adequately supported by the government in terms of inputs and implements, resulting in low yields that led to food shortages and chaos on the farms;
- Recurring droughts.

As a result, humanitarian concerns were increasingly raised by both civic and international communities but no action was taken. Instead, the crackdown intensified. Moral justification for international response put pressure on the Government to stop Operation Murambatsvina. Rehabilitation and restitution werecalled, for but to no avail. The social, economic and political dynamics needed serious review to include the marginalized poor, healing the wounds and halting society from further fragmentation.

Taking Stock of the Operation

By July 2005 according to government sources, a total of 92 460 houses had been demolished directly affecting 133 534 households. The operation also saw a destruction of 32 583 small-macro and medium sized businesses. Based on authoritative studies on the informal economy, an average house-hold size derived from the 2002 census, 5 969 685 people lost their homes and primary source of livelihoods. Resultantly, people suffered.

In the natural order of things, where food, shelter and clothing are competing needs and wants in people's existence and sustenance, there is general agreement that they would rather sleep on an empty stomach with a roof over their heads, than have full stomachs with nowhere to lay their heads for the night. Food, clothing and shelter have been known as basic necessities for human beings since time immemorial and failure to access provisions became an ulcer that affected most victims of Operation Murambatsvina. Many of the victims believed the government had ceased to care about their welfare.

The above statistics do not include those who were indirectly affected by the operation. Several households were also affected indirectly by the disruption of highly integrated and complex networks involved in the supply chain of goods and services that had been established. Those networks included the upstream and down-stream linkages, for example, supply of food stuffs and other goods to, and from rural areas; transport and distribution services; formal and informal micro-credits facilities and a wide range of informal, casual and part-time labour. A reasonable multiplier effect brought the number of indirectly affected people to over 2.1 million.

Interviews conducted at that time, pointed out that the informal sector was totally wiped out. Based on those estimates above, the total population directly and indirectly affected by the demolitions and evictions was 2.4 million or 18% of the total population. Considerable short, medium and longt-term impact to the social, economic and environmental were also experienced.

The education sector also showed that quite a number of pupils of school going age were affected by the operation. School programmes were disrupted as the evictions and demolitions were happening during the middle of the academic year. Roughly, 113 000 children aged between 5 and 11 were affected while 109 000 children aged between 12 and 18 were also affected by the operation. Many displaced children left their school catchment areas to stay elsewhere and in most cases suffered transport problems and lack of money.

On top of it, the teachers who were supposed to monitor pupils and run school activities were not spared by the demolitions and evictions. Several teachers were evicted resulting in them failing to go to work. Ultimately, the quality of education was compromised.

The highly vulnerable groups of Zimbabwean society were not spared too. Such groups included the elderly, children, the sick, the disabled, widows and orphans. The draconian sweep disregarded the plight and needs of these groups. An estimated 83 530 children under the age of four were directly affected by the operation. Already marginalized socially and economically, disadvantaged women and children also suffered a great deal. They became more vulnerable through the immediate loss of homes and livelihoods. Of critical concern however, was denial by the government to allow provision of the humanitarian support for those affected families, leading to increased vulnerability and destitution.

Alluding to the humanitarian suffering Presidential spokesman, George Charamba remarked that Zimbabweans were not "tent people" after NGO's offered tents to the affected people. After such unprecedented turmoil and unleashing security forces to demolish abodes and other structures and condemning thousands of people to destitution and homelessness, the government showed no appetite to provide new accommodation or institute new interventions to ease the plight of the victims. The government spurned the offer of tents stating that there was no humanitarian crisis in the country.

The clear message to be sent to the government was that human suffering could not be ignored at the expense of state sovereignty. That was the stance that previous governments had taken, a stance which the new government had not learnt anything from or conveniently forgotten.

Women had borne the brunt of the war of liberation and this time around they faced the draconian repression from the government which they had loyally supported and voted into power, not only in 1980, but also in subsequent elections.

The clean-up blitz also revealed that 80 percent of at least 10 000 refugees registered by the United Nations High Commission for Refugees (UNHCR), who were staying in urban areas were affected. This was in direct contravention of the official UNHCR policy. Many of these refugees lost their self-reliance jobs making them directly dependent on humanitarian assistance.

Food security, defined not only as the availability of food, but also the capacity to gain access to it through livelihoods, was also under threat. The drought of 2005 had led to a food deficit of 1.2 million tonnes of maize for the 2005-2006 seasons. Bridging the food deficit made it necessary for the country to import food at an estimated cost of between US$250 and US$300 million. At that time, the country was in dire straits, facing chronic shortages of foreign currency and competing for import demands especially for energy, fuel and agricultural inputs.

The situation was worsened by the fact that economic sanctions had also been imposed on the country by the western governments. Zimbabwe thus had no ready access to international credit.

Without heavy external assistance the government subsequently failed to fulfil basic food requirements for the nation. People went hungry because they could not afford to buy the food since their sources of income and livelihoods had been destroyed. The food was also not available on the market, neither was the money to prepare the land and buy agricultural inputs for the next season.

Overall, operation Murambatsvina created a state of emergency, as thousands of Zimbabweans, mainly the poor, were left without protection when their homes were destroyed. The poor were left in the open, without access to adequate water, sanitation, food security or health care. Such conditions were clearly life-threatening.

Economically, Operation Murambatsvina destroyed and seriously disrupted livelihoods of millions of people who were already struggling to survive. In political terms, the operation worsened an already tense and polarised climate punctuated by mistrust and fear.

Operation Murambatsvina Dilemma

The author concludes that Operation Murabatsvina was carries out by government in a reactionary way. He further argues that the event had nothing to do with the 2005 elections or party politics because it hit everyone including ZANU-PF and MDC supporters as well as war veterans. We have, however, to accept a situation of illegal construction of shacks sprouting everywhere had gone out of hand. This was a challenge that required government to dialogue with concerned stakeholders in an effort to seek a lasting solution to the problem.

The issue as to who gave the command to kickstart Operation Murabatsvina remains shrouded in mystery. Many questions are still lingering in the minds of many Zimbabweans. These include concerns such as whether the operation did put to rest Zimbabwe's housing and construction woes. Such questions are not far-fetched and have to be answered by the government so that Operation Murabatsvina will not be repeated in future.

THE YOUTH, SOCIAL, POLITICAL, ECONOMIC INSECURITY AND VIOLENCE

From the statistical data and analysis carried out by different people, there are common factors that converge, indicating that the majority of people who take part in violence are the unemployed youths, mostly males. The holistic belief in, and practice of, abstaining from violence must be taken seriously. Instead of accepting that people from different persuasions may hold conflicting views and opinions without necessarily resorting to violence, fellow Zimbabweans are seen and treated as enemies. Instead of embarking on "nation building and integration", the youths have been drilled to unleash national destruction and disintegration through violence. The principal instrument is the political party whose function is, not only to "articulate" policies that enhance the public good, but also to engage in advocacy for peace, tolerance and national healing.

The bankrollers who sponsor violence are high ranking political elites who are successful in their businesses, but dismal failures in the politics of nation building. They abuse other people's children by hiring them to commit acts of violence against fellow Zimbabweans. Regardless of any party political affiliation, the behaviour of the sponsors of violence is the same. For the political elite, the end justifies the means. No matter the consequences or the costs, including the human life, which is sacrosanct, as long as they achieve their political goals and live in opulence with their families, they will plunder and kill without remorse.

As mentioned earlier, some of the unemployed youths easily become attracted to earn easy money through violence. This is attributed to multiple factors including being coerced into submission by some senior party stalwarts; or by peer pressure from fellow youths due to desire for money; or just mob psychology. The sense of belonging and craving for recognition in the community, are some of the serious contributing factors that influence young people to participate in violence. Systematic destruction of public amenities and vandalism of community utilities which have been witnessed during the times of social, political and economic strife, have something to do with lack of civility and unemployment. The youths may either vent their frustrations on government property or they turn on fellow citizens who may also be victims of political violence.

Zimbabwe society is not the only one which suffers from such hooliganism, but the outcry of the Zimbabwe situation has been made loud and internationalized by the mass media. Sometimes the situation has been blown out of proportions compared to what is happening in other countries, where heinous crimes are committed which are far worse than in Zimbabwe. Yet those countries do not receive the negative media publicity like what Zimbabwe gets. Whether Zimbabwe receives inaccurate or unfair media coverage, locally, regionally or internationally criticism the fact remains that whatever ill-treatment is done to a fellow citizen by anybody, it should be stopped. The tendency to resort to violence when things do not go according to plan is certainly there in our society. Violation of the rule of law in Zimbabwe, by Zimbabweans, towards fellow Zimbabweans happens in more frequent doses than one would expect from a society which boasts a 92% literacy level rate. Of what use then is the high standard of education in Zimbabwe if its people turn to violence at the slightest provocation?

One expects civility (unhu), understanding and appeal to common sense in times of crisis and hardship. It is possible for the people of Zimbabwe to discipline ourselves and resort to dialogue, debate and appeal to reason like what modern societies do across the globe. As a nation Zimbabwe can do it, since we take pride in being the principled nation which makes a firm stand in regional and international issues. Zimbabwe still has remnants of humility and discipline to return to its former glory with its peace-loving, polite and respectful people.

Way Forward to Peace

The 2005 legislative elections were held under a peaceful atmosphere that one wondered why this type of tranquillity had not been upheld during all the previous elections. Even though there had been disagreement over the outcome of the results of the polls, at least there was no violence.

As a way forward, this culture of greater understanding and tolerance of the existence of different political views among people should be permanently sanctified as the only way of exercising citizens' rights to vote at any given time.

It is imperative that the nation should take into account the amount of preparation by government and Non-Governmental Organizations (NGO's) in order to educate the leadership of various political parties, the youth and the general public to abstain from violent behaviour. The conferences which are held with various stakeholders on the initiatives of The Centre for Peace Initiatives in Africa (CPIA) are good peace initiatives that in calculate a peaceful culture in Zimbabwe.

Access to information and its accurate dissemination to all citizens is a fundamental right and the necessary training in leadership skills, especially to the leaders of various youth groups, which requires continuous and rigorous training. The nation should not wait to commence the training programmes just when an election is due.

False and Empty Promises Beget Violence

As part of the way forward for Zimbabwe it is paramount to draw attention to the use of proper and appropriate language by public leaders. Promising the general public something, which will never happen dampens the spirit trust and self -confidence among members of the public. Adults feel very humiliated and betrayed for being treated like children who can be silenced by being told fairy tales of paradise to come soon and all the people living in stupendous wealth happily ever after.

Deliberate and unfulfilled promises are a serious affront on people's dignity. Political leaders should be reminded of the sacredness of promises made to the people. A culture of apologizing to the public when something has gone wrong or when a promise has not been fulfilled, signifies poor leadership. In turn, people will not resort to violence even when they are provoked even in the midst of challenges. Hate language should be avoided by national figures at all costs. It behoves to all and sundry that injustice and impunity can never lead to lasting peace. If injustice is left dangling, it will only harden the wounds that will result in more violence.

Law Enforcement Arms of Government

The law enforcement arms of Government play an important role to curb the use of violence in Zimbabwe. They should be seen to uphold the rule of law and peaceful coexistence without fear or favour and resist political pressures that force them to be partisan, especially during the times of campaigning for elections.

Anyone who is implicated in violent behaviour or proved to be instigating violence and intimidating fellow citizens, should be shamed and brought to book and face the consequences regardless of their political or social status.

A practical example is what happened in December 2004 when one Minister, a senior figure in the party, who was implicated in a violent clash with a budding politician from his own party who had challenged the veteran politician during primary elections. Publicly, the Commissioner of Police stated that according to police investigations, the Minister had a case to answer but the matter died a natural death and the Minister went scot-free. The majority of Zimbabweans who followed the case were relieved by the stance taken by the police because justice was not only being served but seen to be done. Many different communities in the country applauded the Police Commissioner because he had sent a clearsignal that violence during elections would not be tolerated.

Political heavy weights and political policy makers normally set the pace of political behaviour for their followers. So discipline and civic education has to be instilled by the political leadership of the different political parties.

Civic education is a tool which the country has not used to develop the country since the beginning of colonialism. Unfortunately, previous colonial regimes and the Government of an independent Zimbabwe have never taken civic education seriously. Civic education has not been included in the formal school curriculum to educate the pupils from a tender age. Consequently, there was continuous fighting, suspicion, mistrust, racism, tribalism and regionalism because there was no set standard of acceptable behaviour. Therefore, Zimbabwe should introduce civic education into schools from primary school to university levels.

Teaching students political science at university before they have received practical academic background at primary and secondary levels does not make sense. In fact, most people who choose to study political science understand the subject in theory only. It follows that civic education and leadership training should go hand in hand.

The need to rebuild strong civic institutions and grounding children in civic education is the only way to achieve peace and tranquillity. For this to happen, it must start at the community level to groom people in order to achieve greater understanding and peace.

USE OF VIOLENCE AS AN ELECTORAL TOOL IN ZIMBABWE

Since independence in 1980, the use of politically motivated violence as an electoral tool appears to have become an acceptable systematic approach to campaigning for elections by the major contesting political parties even within the same party intra-party violence has been seen, be it at cell, branch, district, provincial or national level, violence and intimidation have been the weapons of choice to win elections. The use of this violence reached its peak prior to, during and after the 29 March 2008 harmonized election and during the run-up to the presidential run-off polls.

The then ruling party Zanu-PF faced the most serious challenge to its continued existence when a nine months old opposition party, the MDC, won almost half of the contested seats in the June 2000 parliamentary election. This Chapter points out the main electoral contestants, their major campaign strategies, their methods of electioneering and their electoral fortunes. It concludes by noting that, within Zimbabwe, the resort to political violence as an electoral tool has encouraged intolerance and thrown the nation into politicosocio and economic turmoil.

Background of the Main Contestants

Elections have been held regularly and on time in Zimbabwe since 1980. In the first independence elections of 1980, Zanu-PF won 57 of the 80 contested parliamentary seats, PF-Zapu won 20 seats and Muzorewa's UANC (United African National Council) won three seats. More than anything else for the local people, it was a vote for peace. Whites whose seats had been reserved by the Lancaster House Constitution had 20 seats for seven years. The shock for the whites in 1980 was all the more profound because they had been convinced that either Muzorewa would win or at least an anti-Mugabe coalition would be possible. In their minds they dreaded a black Marxist government as it seemed one was upon them. Within a short period of time, civil service resignations poured in; and most white families overreacted by leaving the country for South Africa and other far away destinations such as New Zealand and Australia.

In the 1985 parliamentary polls, PF-ZAPU got 15 seats and ZANU-PF got 63 seats. It has to be noted that ZANU -PF and PFZAPU political roots are embedded in the liberation struggle for independence and the guerrilla war which both parties fought to emancipate the country from colonial oppression. Many of their senior leaders belonged to the generation whose political experiences were built in the national struggle. In the following years, the then ruling party saw its representation being increased at the expense of its opponents, whilst electoral participation in elections, drastically declined in successive elections. Violence, intimidation, torture, rape and murder also became rampant. Those in position of political influence failed to act in defence of human rights as well as peace and stability. Supporters of all political parties will continue girding their loins in the various rural, resettlement areas, urban and mining areas if the responsible authorities do not move the local populace from a culture of violence to that of peace and prosperity.

In 1987 following the Unity Accord between the liberation movements ZANU-PF and PF-ZAPU the Constitution was amended to introduce the Executive Presidency and remove the reserved white seats. A unicameral Parliament with 120 seats and 30 presidential appointees was also set up. In the subsequent parliamentary-polls, ZANU PF won 116 of the contested seats and in 1995 it won 117 seats. However, the plebiscite was marred by violence especially in the Midlands Province where a prominent businessman the late Patrick Kombayi, who had resigned from ZANU PF and joined and campaigned for the new FORUM party was shot. The head of security for first Vice President, the late Simon Muzenda committed that offence. He was convicted by the courts and sentenced to jail along with a local ZANU PF Youth League member. Surprisingly, and to the chagrin of many Zimbabweans, and the international community, they were pardoned by a Presidential Decree in 1994. Other former ruling party youths who had also committed violent crimes related to the elections were also pardoned. Several election-related political violence cases never reached the Courts or if they did, the judgments were biased. It was during that period that the then ruling party boasted that it was the only party with "degrees of violence." And surely, the Youth and Women's Leagues were deployed to harass and intimidate perceived opponents and ordinary civilians.

1995 also marked the emergence of the first independent candidate to challenge ZANU PF. Margaret Dongo the Zanu-PF Member of Parliament for Harare South was thrown out of the party citing her outspoken criticism in Parliament. She responded by standing as an independent candidate. She lost the election but won the re-run by-election after successfully taking Zanu-PF to Court for election rigging. The election and by-election were marred by violent attacks on Dongo's supporters.

February 1999 saw the formation and emergence of the MDC to challenge the then ruling party during the 2000 election. The MDC was born out of the Zimbabwe Congress of Trade Unions (ZCTU), the National Constitutional Assembly (NCA), alliance of civic organisations, lawyers, groups representing human rightsactivists and journalists that had united to campaign for constitutional reform. The aim of this broad coalition was to advocate for electoral reform to be in place by the time of the next parliamentary elections in 2000. The coalition also continued with the opposition stance of the ZCTU to the then ruling party's constitutional reform initiatives. The NCA was tasked to spearhead drafting of a new constitution, which would reflect the preferences of ordinary people, as opposed to the Lancaster House Constitution. When the MDC was formed, the wedge between the War Veterans and ZANU-PF political elite was widening. The business sector, commercial farmers and civic society were seen as the main proponents of the MDC.

Under conditions of acrimony, hatred and suspicion, ZANUPF countered the activities of the NCA by initiating its own exercise for constitutional reform. In April 1999 a Constitutional Commission was set up by the government. That Commission was given the task to come up with a new Constitution, which was to be put before the electorate in a national referendum. The draft Constitution was subjected to a referendum held on 12 and 13 February 2000. The MDC, NCA and ZCTU campaigned for a No Vote. The Constitution was subsequently rejected by 55 percent of the voters. The turnout was low. About a one-quarter of the electorate voted: 1 312 738 out of a possible electorate of 5 million. Most of those who cast the "No" vote were from the urban areas. In Harare for example, the ratio of the "No Vote" was 3:1. Most voter surveys and observers suggested that the generality of the public were unwilling to support the document because it was flawed. The voters felt that the document, which they had not seen had been imposed on them.

According to Zanu-PF; "the result was heavily influenced by

the whites". As time went on, the anti-white rhetoric intensified so that in the party's propaganda, the former commercialfarmers became the "enemy of the people".

Zimbabwe's woes, started soon after the rejection of the Constitutional Review Draft during the referendum held on 12 and13 February 2000. This is because violence had emerged during the preceding Constitutional review exercise. The violence was however, spontaneous and not coordinated. The results of the referendum reflected the ebbing fortunes of the ruling party that had been at the helm of political power since independence in 1980. During that period, it was clear that the dominating negative expression against the government supported Draft Constitution included a sizable protest vote. That is when, why and how the phenomenon of violence emerged.

The protest vote was an indication of dissatisfaction with some of the policies that were being followed by the government. Above all, the plight of the ordinary people was increasingly desperate. Poverty, corruption, unemployment, hunger and poor health standards were rampant. Inflation had surged to 60 percent. The unemployment rate had risen to about 50 percent. Manufacturing mining and agricultural outputs were falling by the day.

Meanwhile, the rejection of the draft constitution by the electorate was also construed as a triumph by the recently formed MDC. This perception appeared to show the defeat of the ruling party in the coming election held on 24 to 25 June 2000.

The period between the results of the referendum and the June 2000 election saw another bloodbath characterized by ugly scenes of mayhem, torture, rape and murder. Unprecedented political violence as part of campaigning became the norm.

The Land Issue

The Lancaster House Constitution, which had been forced on the nationalists, meant that for ten years, the government could only buy land at the wishes of white commercial farmers unless such land was designated as "underutilized" or required for public purpose. The owner had to be given prompt and full compensation in foreign currency. Conversely, this meant that land exchanges could only be conducted on a "willing buyer- willing seller" basis. Thus the incumbent government was effectively limited to buying poor-quality land that was voluntary offered for sale by the about 4000 white commercial farmers. White land ownership was grossly misappropriated to their small numbers. According to Meredith, by the end of 1979, white commercial farmers owned 39 percent (15.5 million hectares) of prime agriculture whilst 8000 black small-scale farmers lived on 4 percent of the land. The poor peasant farmers who had borne the brunt of the war and numbering four million accounted for 41 percent of mostly arid land. (Meredith, M, 1979)

As most of the productive and prime land was owned by a few white people, three quarters of all land owned by peasants land was located in drought prone areas, where rainfall was inadequate and the population density was very high. In the rural areas, the population density was more than three times that of "white" areas and the number of people residing there surpassed their carrying capacity by about two million people. Land and environmental degradation were worrying problems for the Government. Land degradation was so widespread in many parts of the rural areas and in somecases it had reached such advanced stages that the regeneration process would take several years to restore the soil and vegetation cover.

While the people's government provided most of the social services in the form of education, health care, better working conditions and high wages to the black majority in the early1980s, underlying socio-political and economic problems remainedunresolved. These eventually produced a national crisis. Of these, the land question was the most pronounced as the liberation-struggle had been waged over the land. During the struggle, promises had been made to return the land to its rightful owners.

Historically inequality was then embedded in the Lancaster House Constitution that preserved the status quo of white ownership of most of the fertile lands as mentioned earlier. In an attempt to address this, in 1992, legislation was enacted to address the inequalities. However, land distribution remained slow, and was sluggish and did not produce the expected results. The main reasons for this failure can be attributed to the fact that the whites (who owned land) acted unfaithfully under the willing-buyer willing-seller stipulated in the Lancaster House Constitution. Funds, which had been promised by the donor community at this conference, were not made available.

With respect to funding, the Zimbabwean intelligence, political elite and their sympathizers, firmly believed that the international community (particularly Europe) had failed them and was concerned more with "regime change" than anything else. Thus to these people, there was no genuine and real concern to address the plight of the struggling poor. Thus over the years, when the government passionately appealed to the international community to buy the desperately needed land, the international community failed to pay attention. Even when it was apparently clear that the former tribal trust land (now communal areas) were congested and no longer able to sustain the increasing population, western countries did not provide the promised funds.

The 2000 Land Reoccupation and the Security Sector

It is against the skewed land distribution policy and the restrictions of the Lancaster House Constitution that on 26 February, 2000, mobs of mostly liberation war veterans violently occupied white commercial farms throughout Zimbabwe. Initially, the ex-combatants of the liberation war, under the auspices of the Zimbabwe National Liberation War Veterans Association (ZNLWVA) did not envisage evicting white commercial farmers violently. However, it was the reaction and behaviour of the white farmers that infuriated them. In the end, the land occupations escalated without options of dialogue. Implementation of reoccupation was entrusted to the war veterans and other unnamed structures while partially disabled the policing functions of the security agents. Masses of activists, and youths began to unleash violence on mainly white commercial farmers and their workers. In that way, it was possible to circumvent the neutralising effect of law enforcement agencies. The deliberate suspension of the rule of law by the government allowed chaos, mayhem and uncertainty to reign supreme.

Thousands of the affected farming community personnel, some without any political affiliation were soon seeking refuge wherever they could find it. Violence was also unleashed on the teachers and nurses in the rural areas. As the wave of political violence gripped the country, the exodus of teachers was witnessed in a number of districts throughout the country. The onslaught on teachers was launched because of the role that they play in society. Teachers are seen as role models, agents of change, sources of information and trendsetters. Because of their educational background, teachers are critical because they are able to analyze political issues and influence public opinion thereby making them targets of political violence because they were regarded as vehicles of change by the contesting parties.

According to the Zimbabwe Teachers Association (ZIMTA), the onslaught on teachers became a great cause for concern and this prompted the teacher's body to appeal to the responsible authorities to guarantee the protection and safety of teachers against political attacks. One headmaster in the Midlands Province said that the situation was so bad if not worse than that which prevailed in the commercial farms. Yet the media had failed to capture those events. In the end, innocent people suffered as qualified teachers sought their safety away from the affected schools. As aptly put by the headmaster, there was no better way of killing the soul of the nation than by destroying the education system. The spectre of violence had negatively impacted on the stability of the Southern African region in general, and Zimbabwe in particular. All in all, those who questioned the timing, legality, management and viability of the fasttrack land reform programme were labelled either sell-outs, stooges of the white farmers or "British agents". They were then subjected to increased harassment, intimidation and violent attacks.

Escalation, Response and Implications

Soon after the constitutional referendum, it became clear that the conditions for free and fair plebiscite, in which parties would campaign freely across the length and breadth of the country and debate issues without fear and intimidation would be difficult if not impossible. Worse political violence was to follow. The result of elections held on 24 and 25 June 2000, gave a knife-edge result to the then ruling party Zanu-PF. The result was not decisive but produced a harbinger. O ut of the 120 contested seats, ZANU PF retained 62 seats with its support coming from mainly rural areas. The MDC attained 57 seats mostly from the urban and western parts of the country. ZANU (Ndonga) retained its traditional seat in Chipinge.

The result left the main contesting parties Zanu-Pf and MDC shocked. MDC fell closely within grasp of the reigns of political power during its first attempt and Zanu-PF was left with the realisation of near defeat. Another development that further entrenched and legitimised the use of politically motivated violence as an acceptable tool in Zimbabwean elections was the passing of the Presidential Clemency Order of No.1 of 2000 in October. The Clemency Order No. 1 effectively provided amnesty and absolution to all those who had perpetrated politically motivated violence against opposition members between January to July 2000. Only those who had committed rape or murder were not covered. Given the ineffectiveness of the law enforcement agencies to function, a perpetrator of violence was not investigated nor brought before the courts.

The message that was sent to victims and their supporters was that the rule of law had been abandoned and all groups had to fend for themselves against politically inspired violence in Zimbabwe. The late Learnmore Jongwe, the MDC's spokesman confessed this assertion as he openly engaged and urged youths and others supporters to "defend their members" in the forth-coming bi-elections that had to emerge as a new battleground for political control of the country. That stance was further reiterated by the MDC party President Morgan Tsvangirai when he announced the recruitment and deployment of 20 000 youths to the Bikita West constituency for the protection of their supporters. Openly the stage had been set for further bloodletting centred on the conduct of elections in Zimbabwe. Thus, leaders from both parties appeared to resolve to continue politicking in order to either maintain the status quo or whistle away the other party's advantage.

Clearly, the immediate impact and implications of the politically motivated violence included regression of economic growth as the country was perceived as characterised by violence, lawlessness and general disorder. The regression of the economy meant people lost their jobs.

These people ended up being potential or fluidly candidates for the recruitment by politicians. Zimbabwe also acquired an image that alienated the international community and lost credibility with key economic funders such as the International Monetary Fund (IMF), World Bank, European Union (EU) and the United Nations Development Programme (UNDP). Middle powers and Scandinavian states like Norway, Sweden, Denmark and Holland also lost faith on Zimbabwe. Thus investors were scared away.

No new production plants were opened neither were the old ones adequately maintained and serviced.

Political Violence and the 2008 Elections

Throughout 2008, Zimbabwe's political terrain was marred by violent preparation and anticipation for the watershed 29 March Harmonised Elections and its bloody aftermath, which resulted in yet the bloodier 27 June run-off election. Both sides of the main political parties were engaged in political violence. In some rural areas ZANU (PF) had established basis where people were reportedly tortured by youth.

In the rural areas bases were set up mostly by ZANU PF, but also by MDC. Party thugs operated illegal road blocks especially in the rural areas. In some instances passengers travelling to their rural homes were harassed by these thugs. The situation got out of hand to the extent that there was no coordination and control of their activities. Subsequently, peasants and travellers to these areas were subjected to some of the worst forms of intimidation and harassment if they failed to recite the party's "current" slogan at the check points.

Events after the botched run-off election marked the "point of no return," which resulted in the formation of the "Second Republic" which was ushered in by the 21 July 2008 Memorandum of Understanding (MoU) that led to the signing of the Global Political Agreement (GPA) of 15 September 2008. As had been in the past, events in 2008 were marked by high tension and more politically motivated violence. However, the intensity, brutality and callousness of violations surpassed all years.

These events seemed as if the country was on the verge of an interncine war. Accumulatively, the total number of murders, assaults, displacements, disappearances, kidnappings or abductions and violations of the freedom of expression, reached the peak point in 2008. However, as stated earlier, leaders from both parties appeared to resolve to continue politicising in order to either maintain their status quo or whistle away the other party's advantage.

This time, the stage was now shifted to the regional level (SADC) where the former president of South Africa Thabo Mbeki was chosen to mediate among the three contesting parties, the MDC

(M), MDC (T) and ZANU (PF). Political tension in the country was drifting without a social contract in place because the country no longer enjoyed tripartite harmonious relations between the State, Labour and Business. That understanding is a precondition for economic stability, which has shied away from Zimbabwe since the late 1980s.

Another weapon that continued to be used during the peak

of violence was the destruction of property. Political thugs torched homes, demolished and stole livestock in rural areas. In the urban areas, buses, cars and some houses were destroyed. The destruction of properties seemed effective as strategy and in most cases dealt a double blow as the victims ended up without food, shelter and were vulnerable and insecure, leaving them with no option but to flee their dwellings. Resultantly, many people failed to vote in their constituencies.

Many of the internally displaced people slept in the open, exposed to the cold, insects and were vulnerable to further victimisation by thugs from the contesting parties. Depending on their location, the affected population was in immediate need of food, blankets, tents, water, sanitation and medical supplies. Most households, which had been hurriedly set up absorbed the evictees. However, in most cases these houses were congested and continuously harassed by security agents. Above all, there was a special need to protect and assist women and children and vulnerable groups such as orphans, the chronically ill and the disabled.

The elections also saw the gender dimensions of politically motivated violence. Gross violations of children's and women's rights were rampant. Many of the perpetrators of these crimes in most cases went unpunished. The message sent to victims and their supporters was that the rule of law had been abandoned and all groups had to fend for themselves against politically inspired violence in the country. The fear for further victimization led to the victims not reporting to the police.

While there was an urgent need to address the humanitarian crisis emanating from politically motivated violence, there was an equally urgent and compelling need to move all the people from a culture of violence to that of peace. Firstly, the humanitarian crisis was not caused by war or conflict. In some instances, it was caused by policy failure on the part of the government to come to terms with rapidly changing political, economic and social environment. These changes had chaotic manifestations.

Secondly, the human suffering resulting from the violence was not caused by mere negligence alone. It had its roots in historical, economic, political and social imbalances, which had their roots from the early 1890s. Thirdly, the effectiveness of any humanitarian response in terms of getting to those mostly affected by the violence, depended almost entirely on instilling a climate of hope and trust between and among all the political parties. Zimbabweans needed to dedicate themselves to putting an end to divisions, intolerance, conflict and polarization, which had characterised politics and society starting from the early 1890s.

Concerned about the challenges mentioned above, the three main political parties agreed to and executed a Memorandum of Understanding (MoU) on 21 July 2008. The MoU amongst other issues agreed to:

- Restore economic stability and growth;
- End sanctions and restrictive measures;
- Resolve the land question;
- Come up with a new and people oriented constitution;
- Encouraged equality, national healing and coercion, respect of national institutions and events;
- Encourage free political activity;
- Respect the rule of law and the Constitution;
- Encourage the impartiality of state institutions and organizations; and
- Promote security of persons and prevention of political violence.

It was against this background that the GPA was signed,

ushering in the Second Republic and a new era of hope, peace and development in Zimbabwe.

In Search of Peace – the 2013 Elections

The brutality of the 2008 elections deeply touched all Zimbabweans across the political divide. What took place in 2008 had never happened throughout the history of Zimbabwe or even during the Rhodesian era. No elections had ever been rerun due to political anomalies or violent conflict. This was the first time and it shook many.

The 2008 election violence caused psychological pain and was also at a great cost to human life and the economy. The country was in a position where investment was impossible. Those with the means to invest could understand, hear and see for themselves the unfolding saga of conflict-riddled elections. No one was immune to the problem. Peace was gone. It was broken.

While the people who suffered most were those at the receiving end of violence, the political parties also realised that it did affect them. Violence can erode a political party's support base and can also make potential voters fearful for their lives. The government too realised the seriousness and tragedy of having violence before, during and after elections. It had to deal with the financial implications of holding two elections – first the harmonised elections and then the presidential re-run.

There was also the unforgettable and emotionally draining experience of having to deal with those who lost loved ones, those who were maimed and those who were either morally or spiritually wounded. The government had to face the consequences of violence when would be investors either waited and watched from the sidelines or backed off completely.

From 2009 Zimbabweans across the political divide began to realise that it was important to place value not on inflicting physical or emotional pain on each other but on engaging each other verbally. There was a sudden realisation that as a nation that prides itself in being highly educated that it was time to talk to each other, listen to each other and that fighting was retrogressive. There was an acceptance that it was possible to agree to disagree, express opposing views, express one's feelings or share one's vision, even if the said vision was not widely shared. With the erosion of peace there was now need for dialogue, continuous meetings and even more vital was the ability to listen to each other. Developing a listening ear helped many people across the political divide. Even within the political parties there were internal disagreements that required mature discussion to be resolved.

Over the next four years from 2008 to 2013 enough time passed for Zimbabweans to reflect seriously and to meditate on what had happened in 2008. It gave the people adequate time to map the way forward and start preparing for a violence-free election in 2013. It had to be a different election – a peaceful one. Civil society and many other groups started working on peace building.

The government's security and social sectors also joined in. In the churches where you found both the victims and the perpetrators of violence, people sought God's grace and guidance. There was a thirst to teach each other that fighting was not the solution and that what was essential was not to wish upon one's neighbour evil. Essentially those in churches sought comfort and direction from Christian values.

The Centre for Peace Initiatives in Africa and other groups dedicated a whole year prior to the 2013 elections to prepare for the elections, by bringing together all the different political parties. At the time the country had 29 political parties but by 2013 there were 34. None of the 29 parties wanted a repeat of 2008 so they worked for peace.

The Centre for Peace Initiatives in Africa took the political parties through a programme on the various stages of an election, the meaning of an election and the importance of respecting each other's choice and political opinion. The idea was to unpack fruitful outcome of an efficiently run election and to assist the political parties to market themselves in a more positive manner, put across their vision and their best teams up for election. It was a time of not just reflection but re-strategising and re-focusing on the real issues that make an election worthy. Instead of simply thinking of landing influential positions, it was time for the various parties to dwell more on which individuals from their parties would make good administrators, professional managers, effective health or education personnel, reliable security staff and sound development leaders.

The Centre for Peace Initiatives in Africa recognised the need and importance of working with all the political parties and ran workshops that had a well thought out programme aimed at adding even more value to a peaceful election. The parties were more than willing to participate and add their voices to a nationwide call for peace. They were all against violence and were determined to nip the scourge in the bud. There was an amazing willingness and commitment to put in as much work as possible towards a peaceful resolution of problems.

In most unstable situations the world over, women and the youth bear the brunt of brutality. This was the same for women and the young people in Zimbabwe in 2008. The women were very vocal during the meetings and spoke about how much they suffered every time there was violence. Women started planning and taking a position on how they wanted to handle matters of conflict right across the country. They wanted to play a significant role.

The youth were also involved in the peace initiative. They were either victims of violence or agents of it. Some of them admitted that they had been involved in acts of banditry, in the beatings or killings at the instigation of some politicians. They felt used and later discarded because when eventually the law caught up with the perpetrators, they found themselves without protection, deserted by the same people who led them into a life of violence. The youth were unhappy with the fact that the people who led them astray kept their own children uncontaminated by acts of violence and abused the youth while they encouraged their own children to go to school or for training in colleges. They expressed dissatisfaction with having to face the music on their own. Some of the youth were drawn into a life of violence because of high unemployment and economic hardship. They were enticed with promises of money, alcohol or food. They stressed during the meetings that they were done with violence and were no longer willing to be used.

Men's sections (male wings) of the political parties also participated in meetings where they pledged to desist from feeding violence. They would no longer take part physically or financially sponsor acts of violence. They challenged each other to work for peace and accepted that they were the driving force behind violence and inflicting pain on each other. These meetings were turning point. There was growing and wider realisation that as intelligent people it made better sense to engage each other in discussion and try and find common ground. They were in agreement that it was normal to disagree but there should be a rational way of solving disputes. Some of the political issues they discussed due to their nature or because of the differences in philosophy of each party there were bound to be disputes.

These disagreements called for rational and intelligent people who saw value in agreeing to disagree while trawling through the disputes to reach an amicable resolution for the greater good and for the development of the country. The meetings created an opportunity for people of different political persuasion to talk to each other, to listen to each other and try and understand each other's point of view. Some of the political parties had similarities in thought and vision while others held totally opposing views. People were able to hear each other out even if they would still not agree on some points, but at least calm discussion prevailed and it paved the way to reach out to the political leadership. Most of the people had pointed out that while they might not want to play a role in perpetrating violence, it was important to get the political leadership to denounce violence so that no politicians would sponsor or encourage it in the future. It was therefore important that the two main and most influential parties be in the forefront of denouncing violence. By the time of the July 2013 elections, President Robert Mugabe of ZANU PF and Mr Morgan Tsvangirai of the MDC-T had since the signing of the Global Political Agreement (GPA) led the government together. They had worked together and it was necessary that they led the call for peace. Their stepping up would ensure that no political party would ever use violence as an electoral tool again.

Fortunately both President Robert Mugabe and Mr Morgan Tsvangirai had more than once condemned violence. The president went a step further, he sent a very strong message to would be perpetrators of violence, that any people who committed violence would be thrown into jail.

The fact that the two party presidents led in denouncing bru-tality, discouraged the use of hate speech and also encouraged their supporters to shun belittling those of a different politic-alpersuasion sent a clear message to all Zimbabweans that the leadership was serious about its proclamation that peace should reign. The leaders called for peaceful electoral campaign, be it through door-to-door meetings or rallies. By voting day nationally and internationally everyone accepted that a calm spirit prevailed. The process before, during and after the election was peaceful.

It was a painful and costly lesson for the nation. Peace came at a huge cost and largely because the people who went through the suffering of 2008, the humiliation and the feeling of being downtrodden had realised that this was not how normal people worked or behaved. Even the perpetrators saw the futility of employing violent tactics as a tool of political persuasion.

It has been proved since time immemorial that violent persuasion might work for a short period but it is not an effective or lasting solution. Brutality visited upon the majority during the Rhodesian era only served to turn more and more people against the minority regime. People might feel terrorised and scared for a while but eventually they gain the courage to say enough is enough. While some might have gained paltry economic relief from their work as agents of violence, it was not a lasting remedy to their state of unemployment or the increasing high cost of living. Clobbering someone on the head will not encourage that person to vote for you or your party.

In the aftermath of the instability of 2008 civil society and the churches through the peace building meetings taught the various players the benefits of learning the art of non-violent persuasive language. Political parties were refocused around real bread and butter issues. They worked hard to convince the people why they thought their parties or leaders were the best, how they would turnaround the country, how they would create employment, reduce poverty, come up with better health care, improve the education system and how they would create an efficient civil service as well as eradicate corruption.

Peace made sense not just to the politicians and their supporters but also the business community. The economy was bleeding and investors were beginning to look at opportunities in neighbouring countries. No one wanted to pour money into an unstable country and the potential investors were merely being rational. It just did not make any economic sense. Business was unwilling to pay for violence and they realised the consequences of a budget aimed at sponsoring violence. Trading in such a commodity spelt the end of their business and they understood this, it was no rocket science.

Holding a peaceful election in 2013 was a huge step for Zimbabwe. Removing conflict was a necessary move. It opened the door for Zimbabweans to finally focus on how they can use their education and skills for the development of the country. Progress requires peace and full commitment from all citizens. Violence impedes development.

For the majority of Zimbabweans the work towards a peaceful Zimbabwe officially started when the MDC and ZANU PF negotiated Global National Unity Agreement. However, the reality is that the two parties had started trying to find common ground as from 200. In 2000 the ruling ZANU PF faced its greatest political challenge in the form of a newly formed MDC. The new opposition had taken the urban areas by storm and made a very good showing in the 2000 general elections.

In 2001 a local initiative for the two main parties to work out a working relationship started under the chairmanship of the writer.

Some of the politicians had gone to school or university together but now found themselves on opposing sides but they knew they could open the lines of communication. No one ever brought a knife or iron bar to the meeting – words were enough.

There was disagreement on several issues and the negotiations broke down several times but they talked and smiled at each other. These meetings made a major difference although it might not seem like that considering that the discussions dragged from 2001 to 2008. By 2001 the outside world was beginning to express worry about the political situation in Zimbabwe. It took a while for people to find out that MDC and ZANU PF were in negotiation. Even former presidents Thabo Mbeki of South Africa and Olusegun Obasanjo of Nigeria tasked by the Commonwealth to find a solution to Zimbabwe's political dispute only found out when they engaged President Mugabe and Mr Tsvangirai that the two leaders had proactively tasked teams to hold talks. Mr Obasanjo and Mr Mbeki were highly impressed when they heard that there was ongoing dialogue between ZANU PF and MDC and they urged the Zimbabwean leaders to publicise it.

The good thing was there was no going back. As is to be expected in any conflict resolution there were some tussles from time to time and periodically there was breakdown of talks then they would suspend for a short period of time to relook at the sticking points. They would renegotiate and they continued until they realised it was essential for the two political parties to meet at a higher level. It was time for the leadership to put its stamp on the talks.

Despite the fact that there had been a progression of negotiations since 2001, the run up, during and after the 2008 the country saw a brutal election campaign. Lives were lost, some were maimed and others lost their homes and livestock. Obviously up to that point the nation had not done enough to discourage brutality and get people to discuss more amicably. The country was still a long way from sustainable tolerance and peace.

The image of broken peace was firmly imprinted on the

minds of all and it was now up to the political leadership of themain political parties to strategize on how to put together a government of national unity. Negotiations gained momentum, which culminated in the Global Political Agreement (GPA). Some made fun of it and did not expect much out of it. It was not perfect but it did bring about peace and stabilised the economy and political situation. Order was restored, the country adopted use of a multi-currency system banishing the Zimbabwe dollar. The shops that had run out of food and other goods once again had well stocked shelves.

On the other hand when the politicians realised that they could work together as a government the tensions started to die down. They now had an opportunity to dispel each other's suspicions, learn from each other and share experience. Suspicions did not automatically disappear but governing together helped restore stability. Those from the opposition who had never governed found out first hand that opposing was easy but getting the various sectors of the economy to function efficiently was no walk in the park. They realised that governing was tough while those with the experience of ruling suddenly realised that they had to be more diligent because there were some people in the opposition who wanted to do better and to achieve more. The MDC was raring to govern and ZANU PF could no longer take anything and the people for granted. Both parties were spurred to show they were up to the job. The Government of National Unity (GNU) is an important part of Zimbabwe's political history.

But 2009 was not the first time the country's political parties had entered into a government of national unity. A similar situation prevailed in 1978 and in 1979 but the only difference with 2009 was that this was for a longer period – 2009-2013. The latest GNU had its own drawbacks but there were also many positive outcomes.

The main lesson to be drawn from this experience is the fact that the lifespan of a country should not, be determined by that of an individual. A country has an indefinite period of life while humans are mortal. Every Zimbabwean should be committed to leaving a meaningful legacy, put a positive dent on the country's lifespan and aim to be remembered with intense love and appreciation.

With peace Zimbabwe can achieve the same levels of superiority that countries which are known as super powers today possess. All the major countries were not born superior it took sacrifice and hard work. For Zimbabwe sacrifice should not be just through the barrel of the gun, but through intellectual and professional sacrifice, commitment to developing the country and putting in place long term plans, plans that go beyond 50 or 100 years. The Zimbabwe of 1870 is a far cry from the Zimbabwe of 1980 and this should be the same for the Zimbabwe to be inherited by future generations. It should be a Zimbabwe that is well developed and a Zimbabwe that continues to grow and flourish. When the world looks at Africa, Zimbabwe should be the centre of the universe. Many look at Europe, Japan, America and China with envy and this should be the same way other countries should look at Zimbabwe.

Zimbabwe has all the necessary ingredients for success – a highly educated, highly skilled population, natural and mineral resources and good agricultural soils but it takes individual and collective commitment to exploit the prevailing peace and knuckle down to the hard work of reconstruction and further development. There must be a common vision that guides the nation, a vision that puts the country ahead of personal interests. The country's high literacy rate must translate into something more meaningful. Time wasted on violence must now be ploughed into ensuring that the country has an enviable future.

Peace has positive spin-offs for the country as a whole. Business can resume in earnest, investors know that because there is stability all they have to worry about is negotiating with the government to ensure that finance and trade policies are investor-friendly. Both security of investment and that of the individual are important to the development of a country. Naturally when there is peace, citizens also have expectations of an improved standard of living, an increase in the availability of jobs and improved money supply. It is crucial that people can talk and walk freely but it is more vital that the people can reap the tangible benefits of a peaceful state.

Viable and sustainable peace is only possible when people can benefit from their education or training. In a country where the US dollar is the currency of survival and doing business, people require the opportunities and the tools to earn the money. Productive people who know their future is assured have no time to waste on violence. People want their own currency, one they are in control of but where that does not exist they need the reassurance that the opportunities of legally earning that foreign money are there.

There have been arguments that violence took root because people were economically impoverished and were hungry. If this was the case then what it requires is to ensure that the nation is well fed and that all triggers of violence are completely eradicated.

Peace should not be taken for granted. Political leaders should ensure that peace is continuously encouraged and nurtured. There should never again be a day when some people fall back on violence simply to earn a meal.

CONCLUSION

Violence and violation have characterized the Zimbabwean political and Socio-economic terrain ever since the 1890s. This has been perpetrated by political parties or in some instances by State institutions and organisations. The results have seen the precipitation of a humanitarian crisis of immense proportions. The impact of the violence among others has seen people being killed, maimed and tortured. The use of violence and victimisation of the people has become an established fact since time immemorial. The subsequent close fighting over political power has resulted in the entrenchment of the practice of violence as a method of either getting into political office or sustaining that power once under threat. The implications point towards a nation characterised by political intolerance, disregard of law and order, economic and social upheaval, and the abuse of the electorate who are held hostage until they cast their vote.

The disregard for laws and international conventions has set a bad precedent in colonial and post-colonial Zimbabwe. Governments and political parties that had wrestled for power have breached national and international human rights law provisions thereby causing division, conflict, polarisation, intimidation, patronage and inequality. Appreciating the historic obligation and the need to resolve the present challenges that will allow political parties to put Zimbabweans first, the government and its institutions should grab the principle of moving the Zimbabwean citizens from a culture of violence and violation to a culture of peace. If this approach is embraced fully, and implemented in full, Zimbabwe would be great once more.

The common point of departure in this study is that violence and violation have had a negative impact on the general populace in Zimbabwe. The State, through its organs and institutions, during and after the colonial era, has reacted to the perceived threat, negatively, and created instruments of violence and coercion. It is against this background that the study attempts to provide insights into how state and party instruments of violence have been established, controlled, reinforced and commanded in colonial Rhodesia and post-independence Zimbabwe. The study results have provided a critical mirror that shows in-retrospect, the rationale as to why policy makers and practitioners have behaved in a particular manner in their quest to get- into, or stay in power.

For many of the victims, the impact of violence has horrendous effects. It is in the interest of all that the culture of violence has to be ended since its effect is not selective. There is urgent need for the prevention of violence and move away from this evil culture. Given these high stakes, alternative measures, whether diplomatic, political or economic, must continue to be pursued vigorously by policy makers in Zimbabwe, to end violence.

In any political situation, stakes are usually high. For any political candidate and their supporters, assuming office means gaining access to power and ultimately control over important resources. It is not the political process itself that engenders violence and violation, but it is the process that leads to conflict. It is important to manage this conflict before it breaks into a fully-fledged war by having responsible and responsive State and democratic political party institutions. The early warning systems should be formulated to detect early forms of conflict and nip them in the bud.

ZIMBABWE NATIONAL ANTHEM

BLESSED BE THE LAND OF ZIMBABWE (ENGLISH)

Oh lift high the banner, the flag of Zimbabwe
The symbol of freedom proclaiming victory;
We praise our heroes' sacrifice,
And vow to keep our land from foes;
And may the Almighty protect and bless our land.

Oh lovely Zimbabwe, so wondrously adorned
With mountains, and rivers cascading, flowing free;
May rain abound, and fertile fields;
May we be fed, our labour blessed;
And may the Almighty protect and bless our land.

Oh God, we beseech Thee to bless our native land;
The land of our fathers bestowed upon us all;
From Zambezi to Limpopo
May leaders be exemplary;
And may the Almighty protect and bless our land.

SIMUDZAI MUREZA WEDU WEZIMBABWE (SHONA)

Simudzai mureza wedu weZimbabwe
Yakazvarwa nomoto wechimurenga;
Neropa zhinji ramagamba
Tiidzivirire kumhandu dzose;
Ngaikomborerwe nyika yeZimbabwe.

Tarisai Zimbabwe nyika yakashongedzwa
Namakomo, nehova, zvinoyevedza
Mvura ngainaye, minda ipe mbesa
Vashandi vatuswe, ruzhinji rugutswe;
Ngaikomborerwe nyika yeZimbabwe.

Mwari ropafadzai nyika yeZimbabwe
Nyika yamadzitateguru edu tose;
Kubva Zambezi kusvika Limpopo,
Navatungamiri vave nenduramo;
Ngaikomborerwe nyika yeZimbabwe.

KALIBUSISWE ILIZWE LEZIMBABWE (NDEBELE)

Phakamisan iflegi yethu yeZimbabwe
Eyazalwa yimpi yenkululeko;
Legaz' elinengi lamaqhawe ethu
Silivikele ezithan izonke;
Kalibusisiwe ilizwe leZimbabwe.

Khangelan' iZimbabwe yon' ihlotshiwe
Ngezintaba lang' miful' ebukekayo,
Izulu kaline, izilimo zande;
Iz' sebenzi zenam', abantu basuthe;
Kalibusisiwe ilizwe leZimbabwe.

Nkosi busis' ilizwe lethu leZimbabwe
Ilizwe labokhokho bethu thina sonke;
Kusuk' eZambezi kusiy' eLimpopo
Abakhokheli babe lobuqotho;
Kalibusisiwe ilizwe leZimbabwe.

BIBILIOGRAPHY

1   Alexander, J, McGregor, J. and Ranger, T. (2000). *Violence and Memories: One Hundred Years in the Ark Forests of Matabeleland.* Oxford: James Carrey.

2   Astraw, A. (1983). *Zimbabwe: A Revolution that lost its way.* London: Zed Press.

3   Beach, D. N. (1986). *War and Politics in Zimbabwe 1840 – 1900.* Gweru: Mambo Press.

4   Beach, D. N. (1987). *Mapondera 1840 – 1904.* Gweru: Mambo Press.

5   Beach, D. N. (1979). *"Chimurenga"* The Shona of 1896 – 1897. In Journal of African History, 20, 3.

ᵣ   Bowman, L. W. (1973). *Politics in Rhodesia: White Power in an African State.* Harvard : Massachusetts.

7   Centre for Peace Initiatives in Zimbabwe. (CPIΛ). (2005). *Zimbabwe the Next 25 Years.* Harare: Benaby Printing & Publishing (Pvt). (Ltd).

8   Chitiyo, K. (1999). *"Land, War and Compensation in Zimbabwe".* unpublished Seminar Paper, Germany: Bonn International Centre for Conversion (BICC).

9   Keppel-Jones, A. (1983). *Rhodes and Rhodesia: The White Conquest of Zimbabwe 1884 – 1902.* Ontario: McGill-Queens University Press.

10 Martin, D. and Johnson, P. (1981). *The Struggle for Zimbabwe: Chimurenga War.* London: Faber & Faber.

11 McLaughlin, J. (1988). *On the Frontline; Catholic Mission in Zimbabwe Liberation War.* Harare: Baobab.

12 Meredith, M. (1979). *The Past is Another Country.* London: Andre Deustch.

13 Nkomo, J. (2001). *Story of My Life.* Harare: SAPES.

14 Phimister,1. (1988). *The Combined and Contradicting Inheritance of the Struggle Against Colonialism; Zimbabwe' Prospects: Issues of Race, Class, State and Capital in Southern Africa.* (ed) Stoneman, London: Macmillan.

15 Raeburn, M. (1978). *Black Fire: Accounts of Guerrilla War in Rhodesia.* London: Julian Friedman.

16 Ranger, T. O. (1970). *The African Voice 1898 – 1930.* London: Heinemann.

17 Ranger, T. O. (1967). *Revolt in Southern Rhodesia.* Heinemann: London.

18 Rupiya, M. (1999) *"Psychological Impact of the War in Zimbabwe: The genesis of the problem and the nature of persisting Post-Traumatic Stress Disorder (PTSD). Towards a national recognition of PTSD amongst ex-combatants from the Liberation war and calls for mechanisms to address the problem".* unpublished Seminar Paper; Germany: Bonn International Centre for Conversion (BICC).

19 Tapfumaneyi, A. W (1999). *Role of the Military in Zimbabwe.* A paper prepared for the Bonn International Centre for Conversion, (BICC) on behalf of the Southern African Research and Documentation Centre, Germany: (BICC).

20 The Holy Bible, New International Version (2007): England, Lux Verbi. BM.

21 Young, K. (1969). *Rhodesia and Independence.* London: Dent and Sons.

22 Zimbabwe Epic (1982), Harare, National Archives

23 Zindi, F. (2010) Music Guide for Zimbabwe, Harare: ZINDISC Publication

ACRONYMS AND ABBREVIATIONS

ANC	African National Congress
BSAC	British South Africa Company
BSAP	British South African Police
EU	European Union
GPA	Global Political Agreement
IMF	International Monetary Fund
MDC (M)	Movement for Democratic Change - Mutambara
MDC (T)	Movement for Democratic Change - Tsvangirai
MoU	Memorandum of Understanding
NDP	National Democratic Party
PCC	People's Caretaker Council
PSTD	Post Traumatic Stress Disorder
PV	Protected Village
RAF	Rhodesian Air Force
RF	Rhodesian Front
RSF	Rhodesian Security Forces
SADC	Southern African Development Community
SAS	Special Air Services
UDI	Unilateral Declaration of Independence
UNDP	United Nations Development Programme
ZANLA	Zimbabwe African National Liberation Army
ZANU	Zimbabwe African National Union
ZAPU	Zimbabwe African People's Union
ZIMTA	Zimbabwe Teachers Association
ZIPRA	Zimbabwe People's Revolutionary Army